The Track Song

by Chelsea O'Brien
Illustrations by Nancy Berg

The Track Song

Cover and Interior Art by Nancy Berg

ISBN: 978-1-939790-59-0

O'Brien, Chelsea
The Track Song/Chelsea O'Brien

First Edition: March 2022

Starseed Books
Douglas, Michigan
An imprint of Lorian Press LLC

Dedication

The Track Song is dedicated to Wally Niezguski whose life's work was spent contributing to organic gardening, environmental stewardship and agricultural education. His legacy scholarship fund for kids at the farm will be a living testament to his passion for growing hearts and minds and beautiful healthy food.

Acknowledgements

The Clarkston Family Farm acknowledges both Chelsea O'Brien and Nancy Berg as well as the farm's curriculum development team for their perseverance, ingenuity and talent in creating sensory and content rich science exploration while incorporating art and music in these interactive and fun lessons.

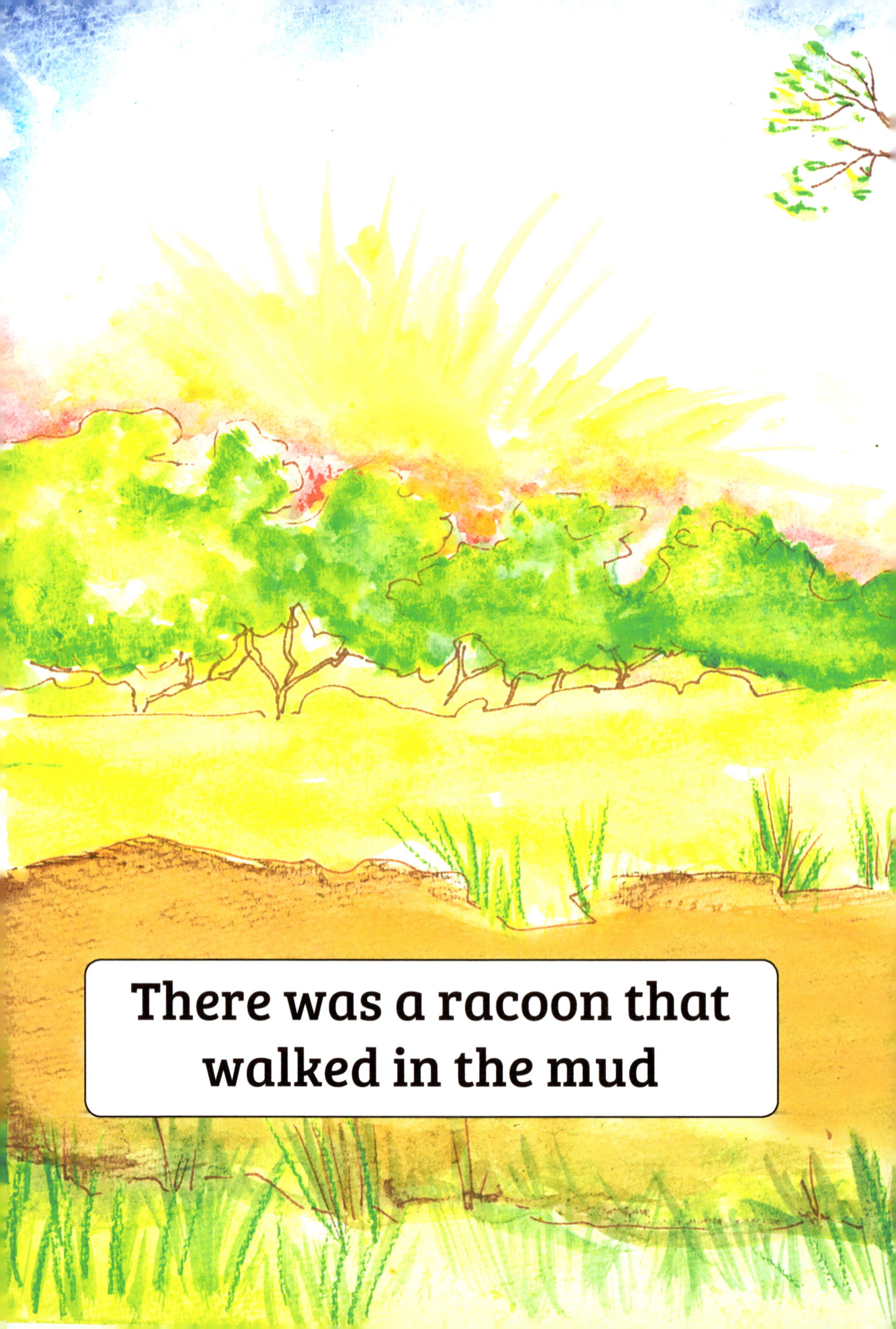

There was a racoon that
walked in the mud

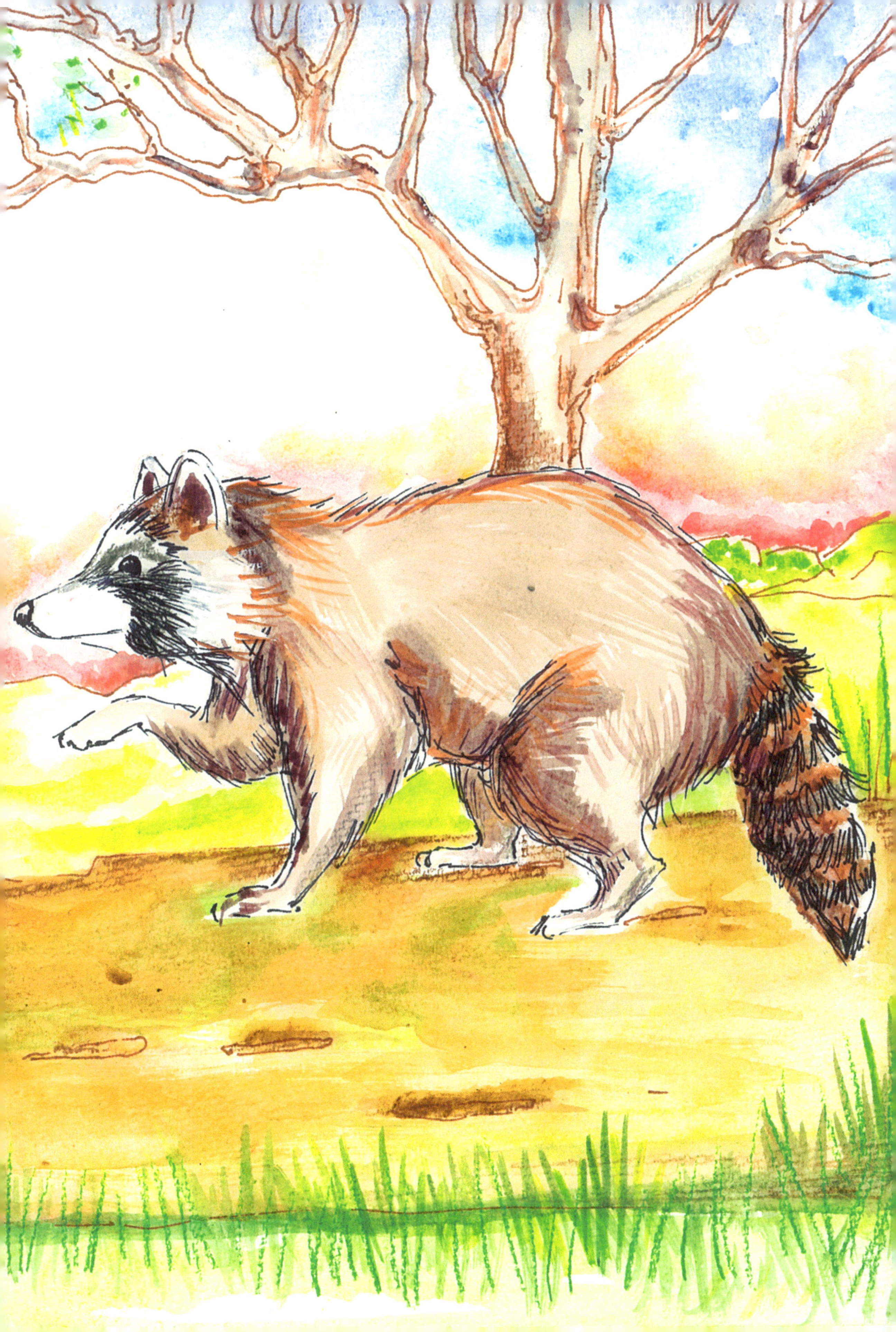

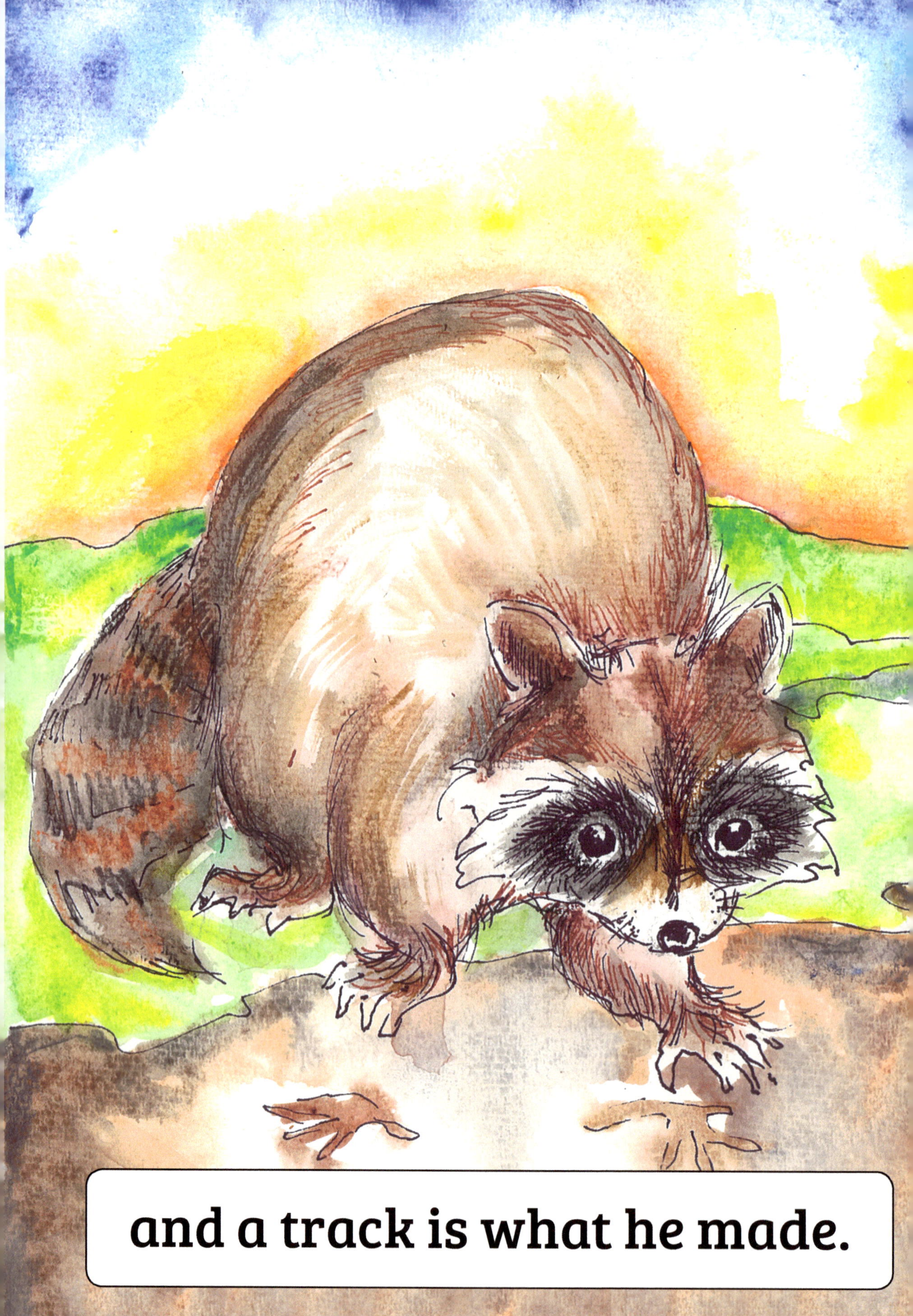

and a track is what he made.

T·R·A·C·K

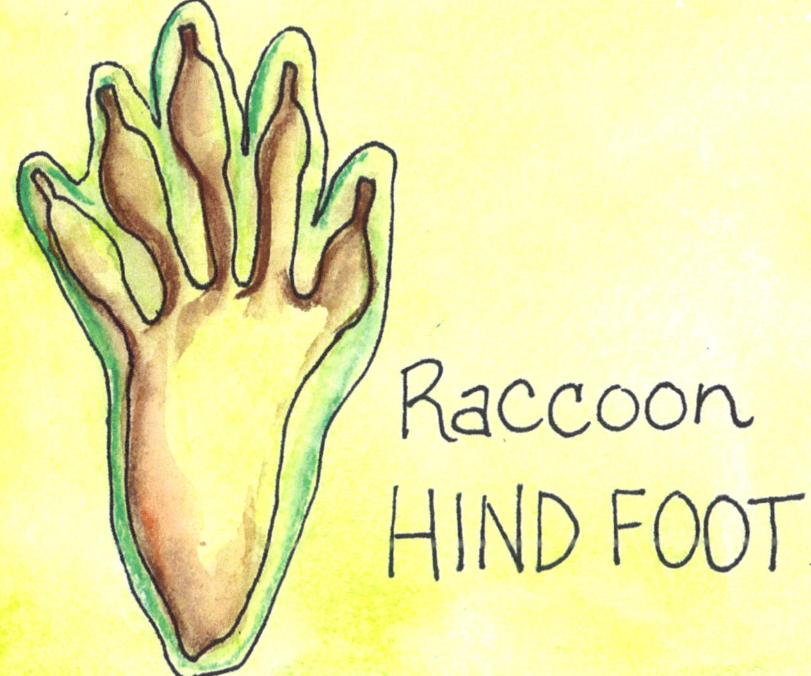

Raccoon
HIND FOOT

T·R·A·C·K

T·R·A·C·K

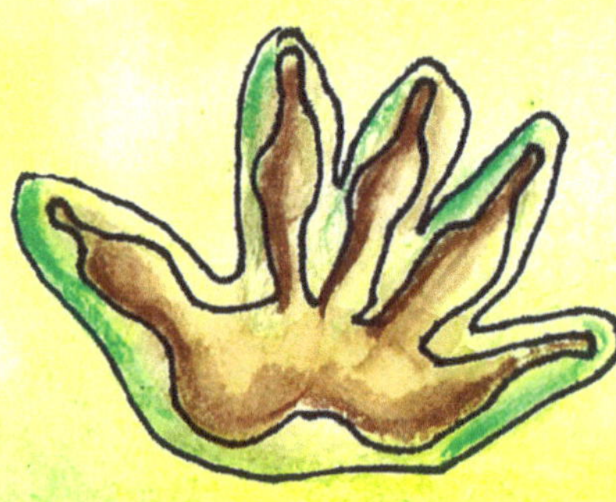

Raccoon
FORE·FOOT

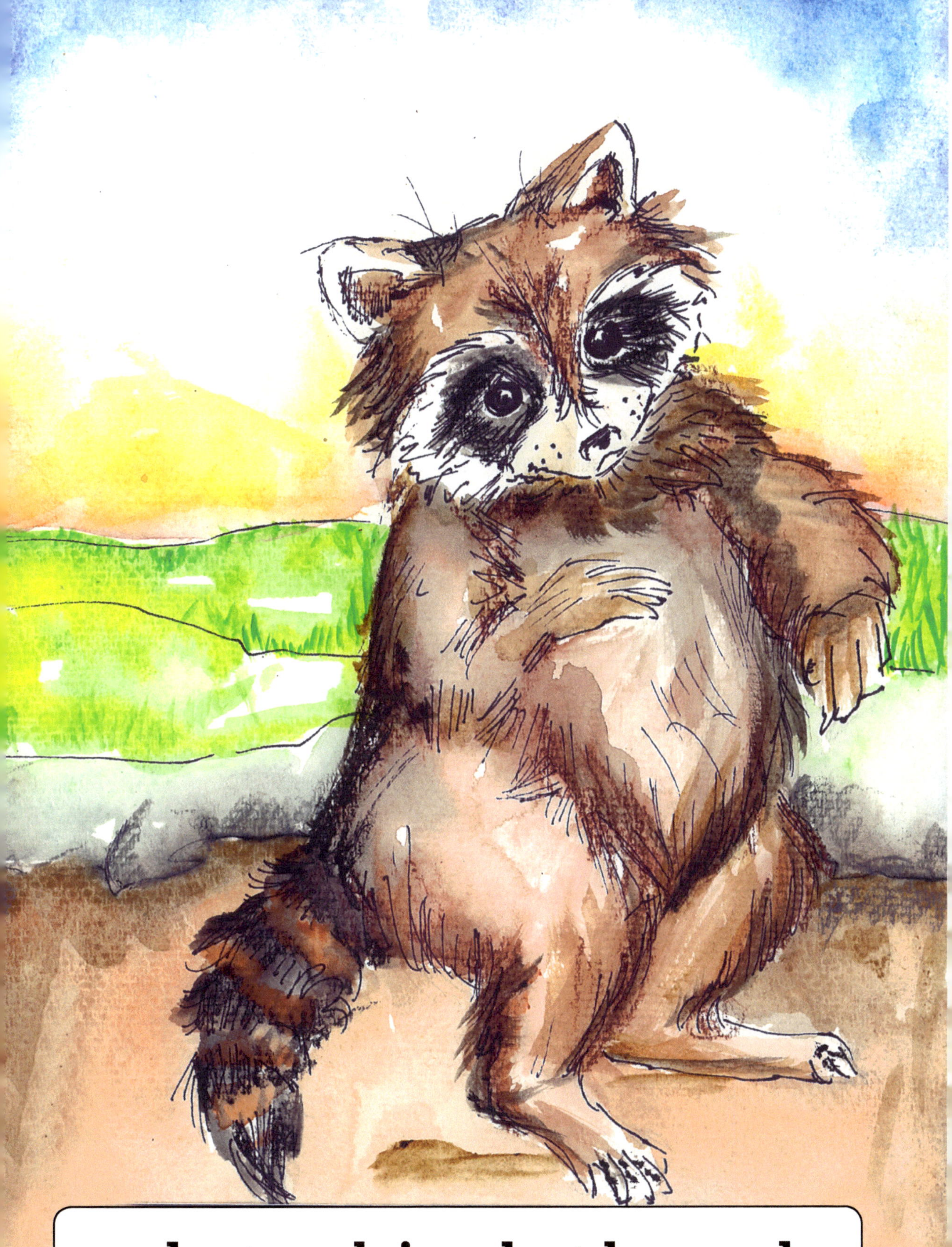

and a track is what he made.

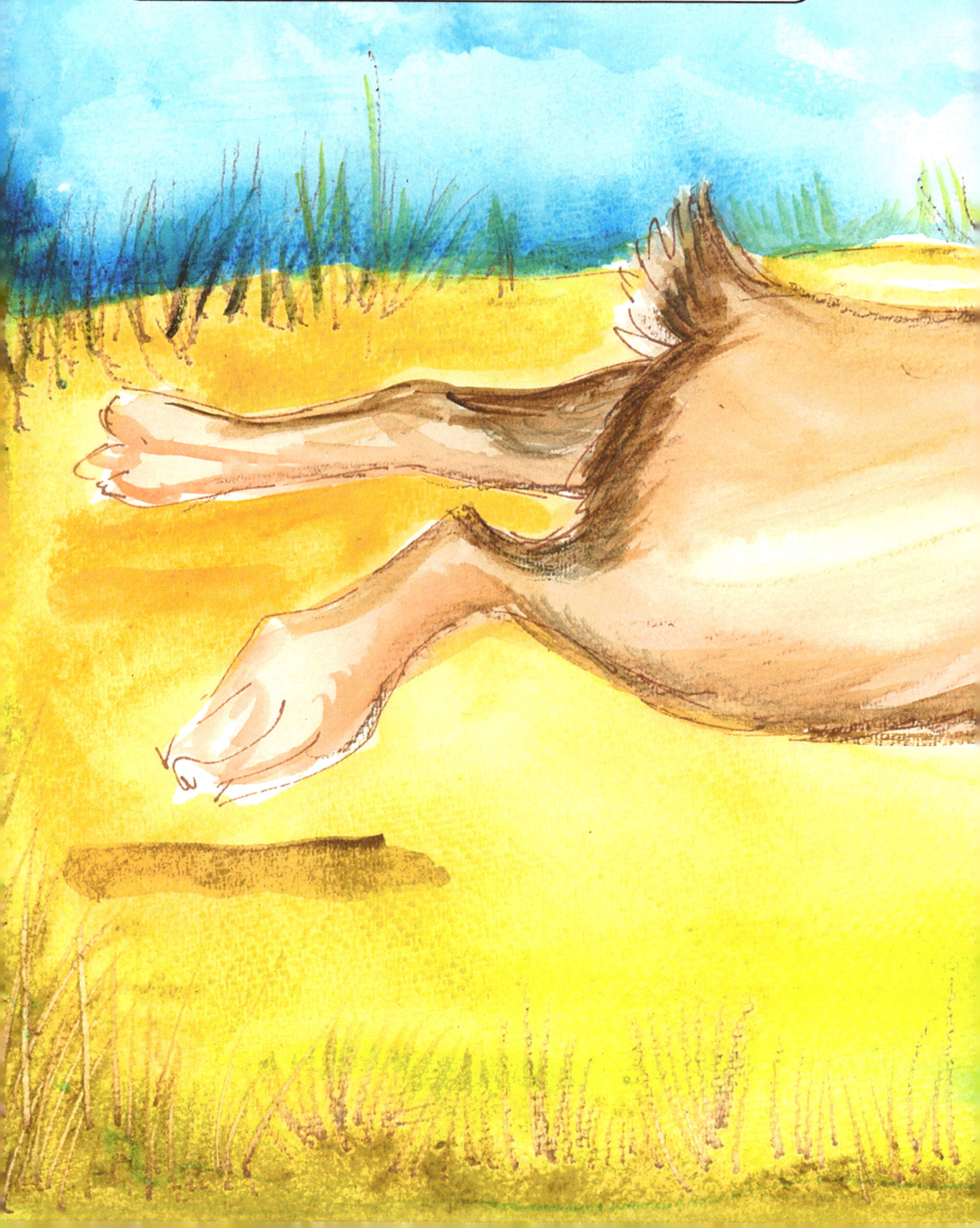
There was a rabbit that hopped in the sand

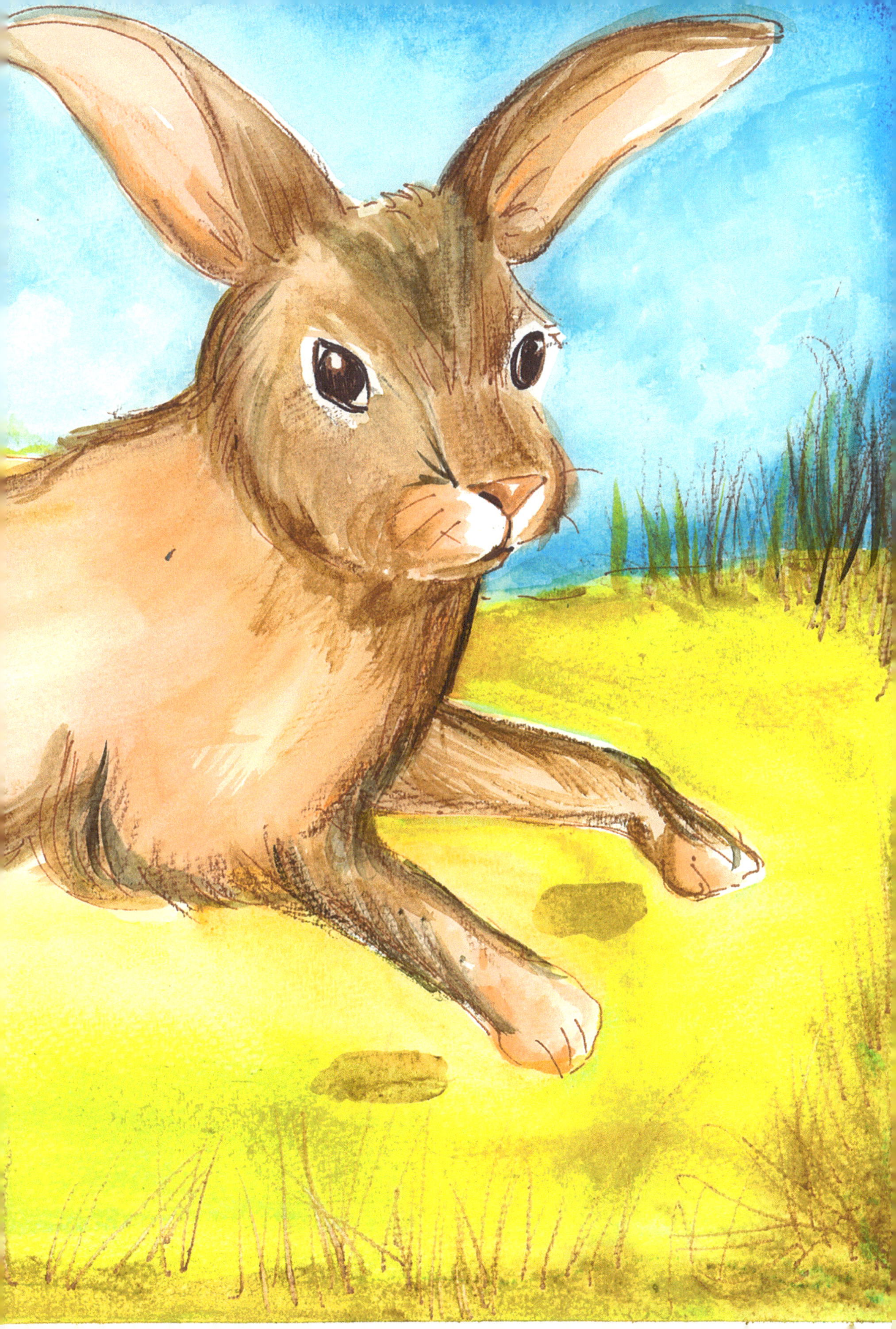

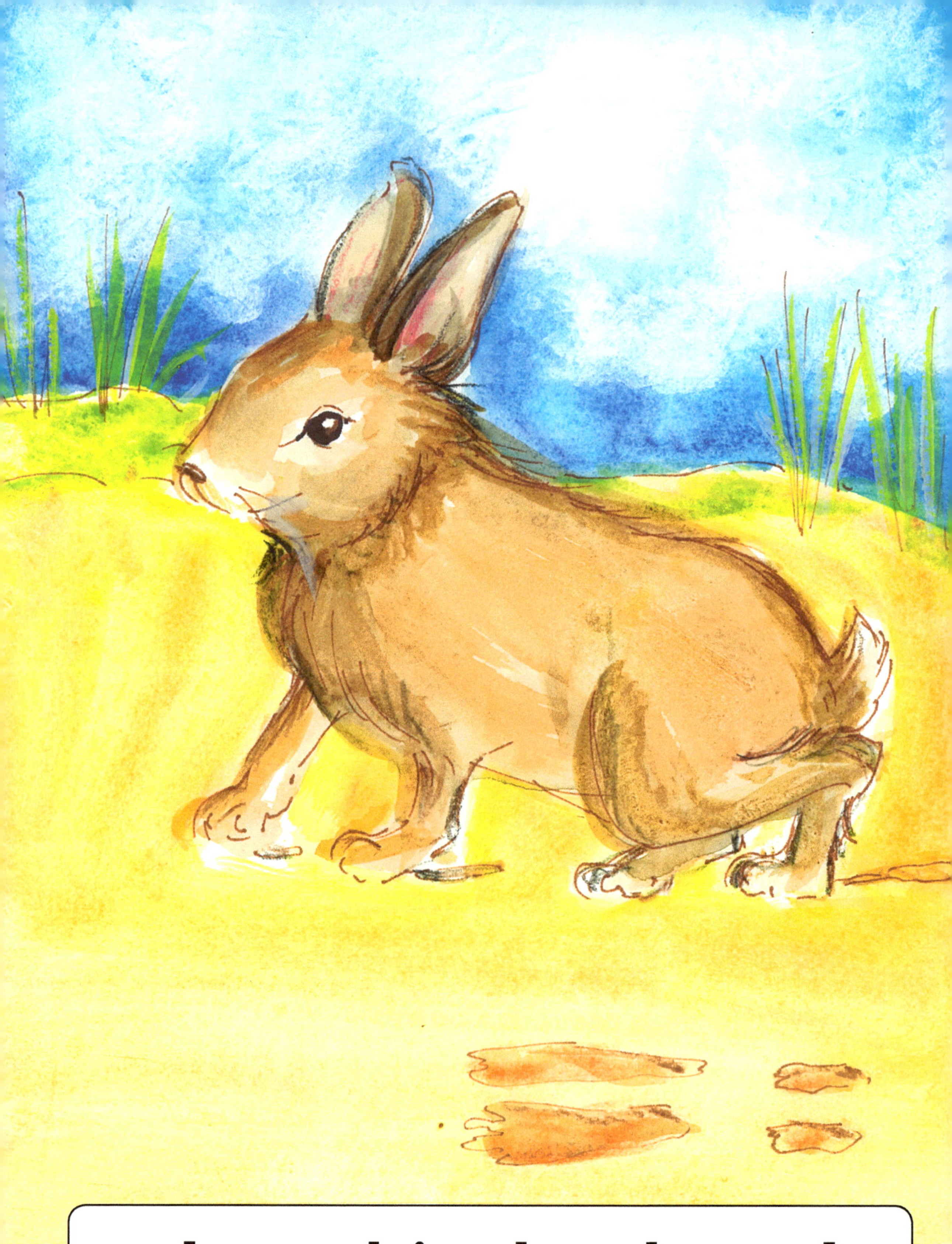

and a track is what she made.

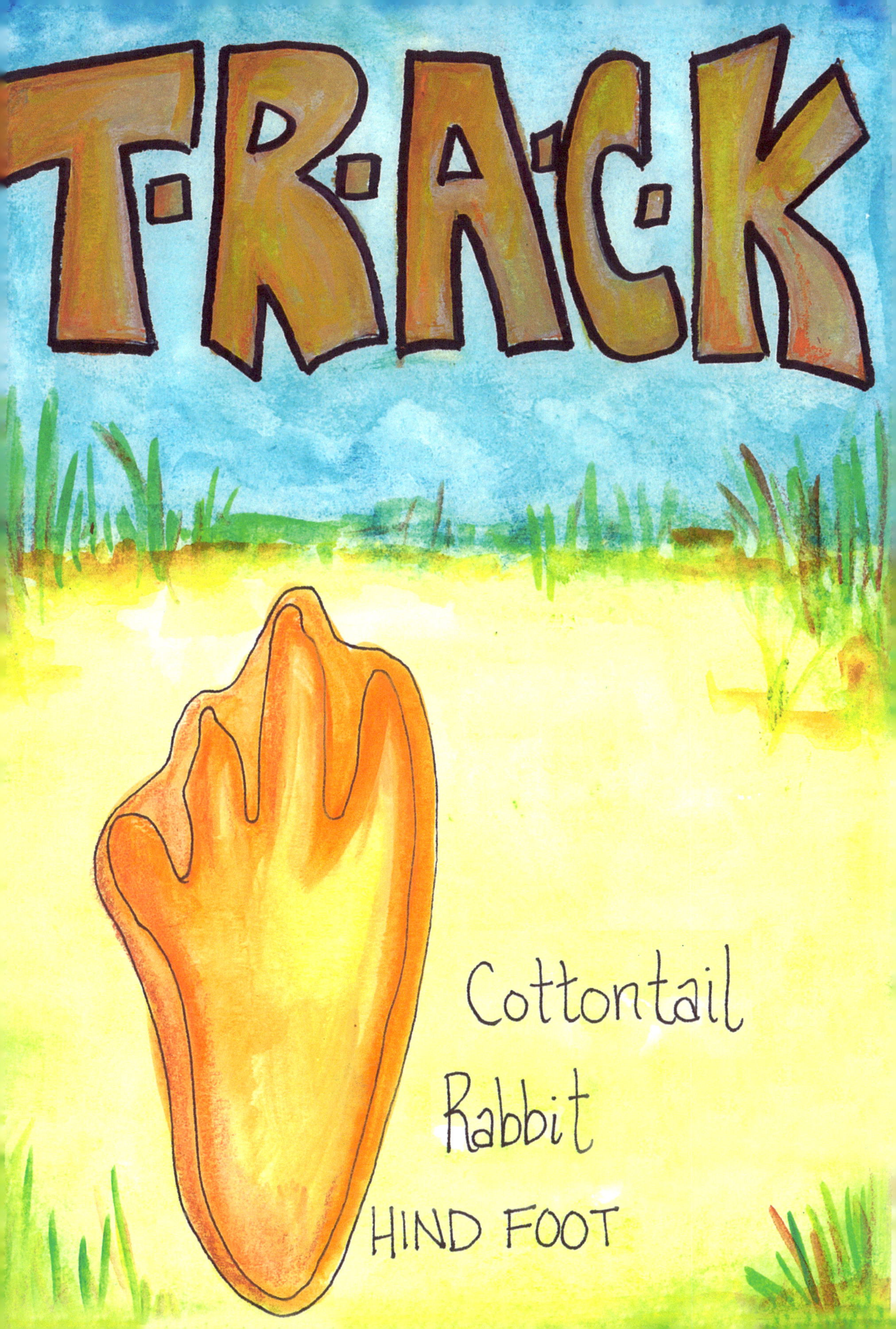

T·R·A·C·K
Cottontail
Rabbit
HIND FOOT

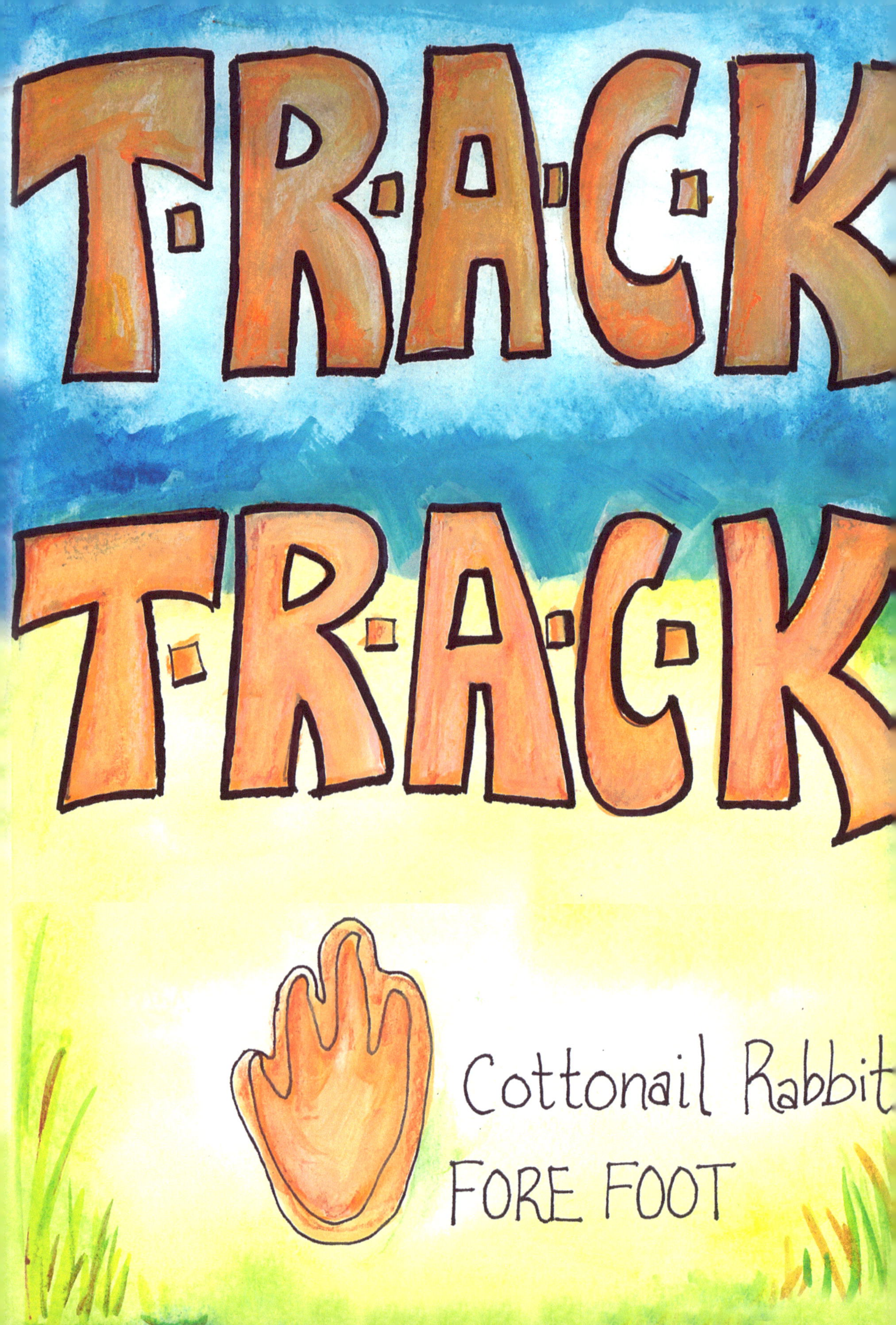

T·R·A·C·K
T·R·A·C·K
Cottonail Rabbit
FORE FOOT

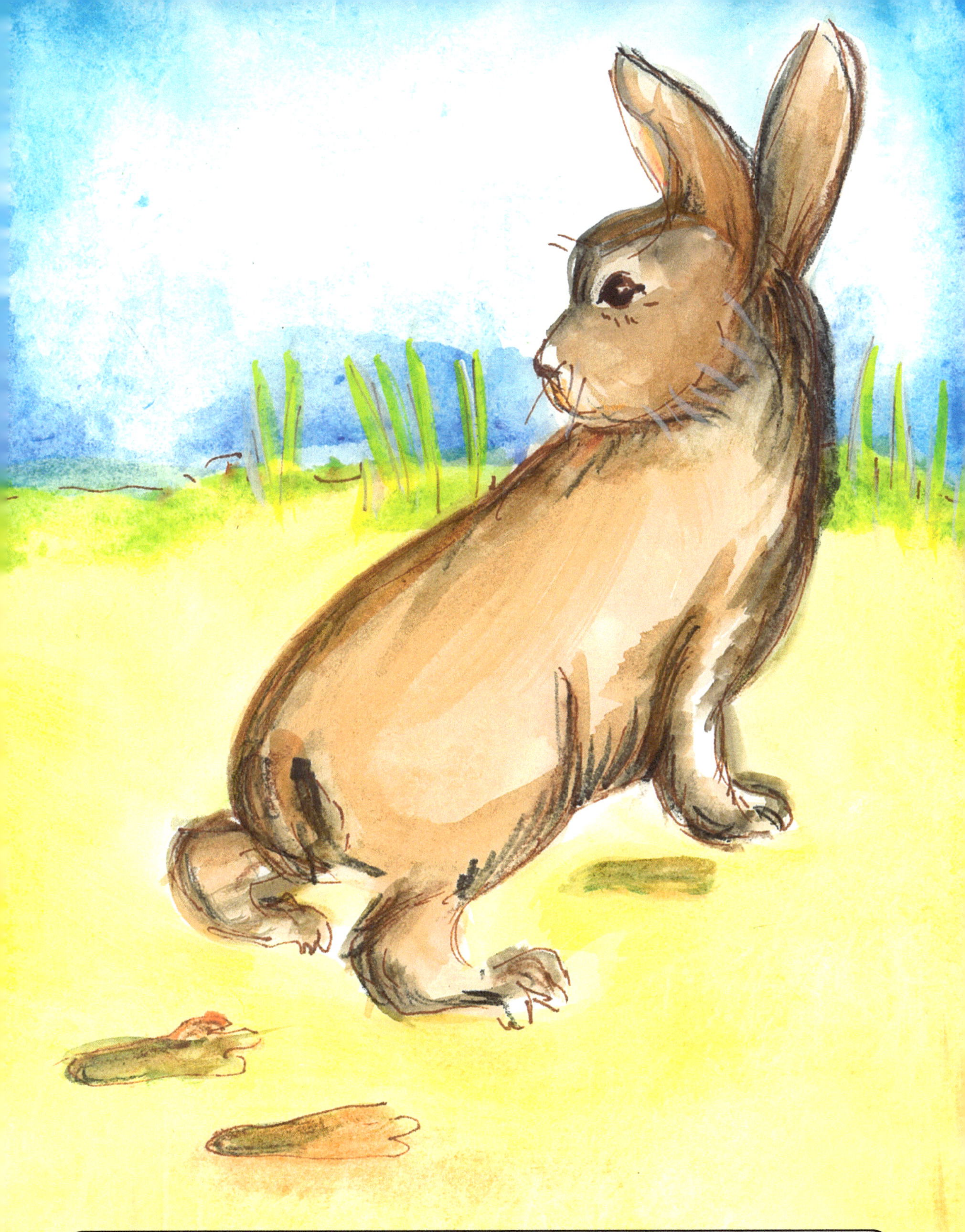

and a track is what she made.

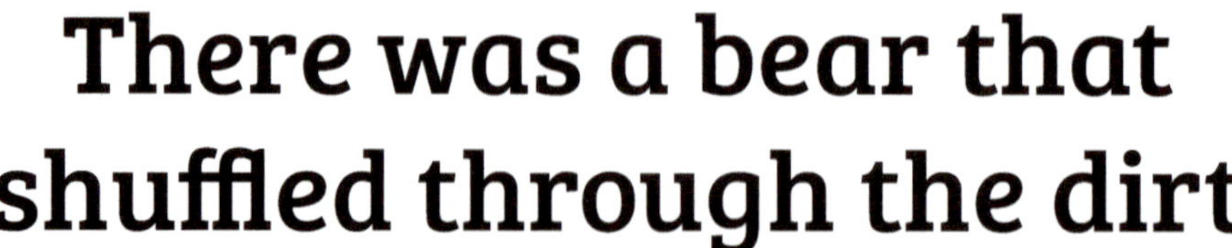
There was a bear that
shuffled through the dirt

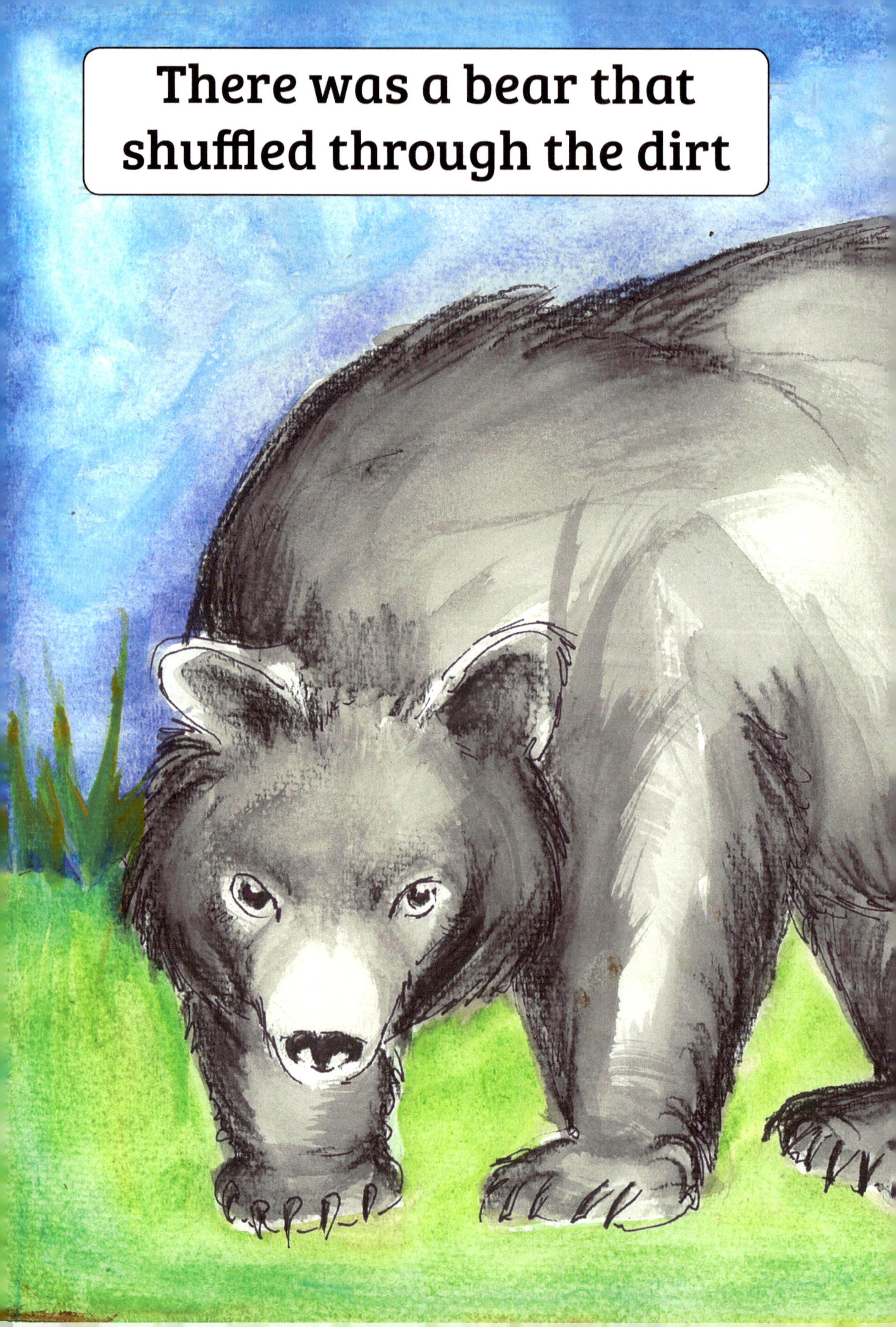

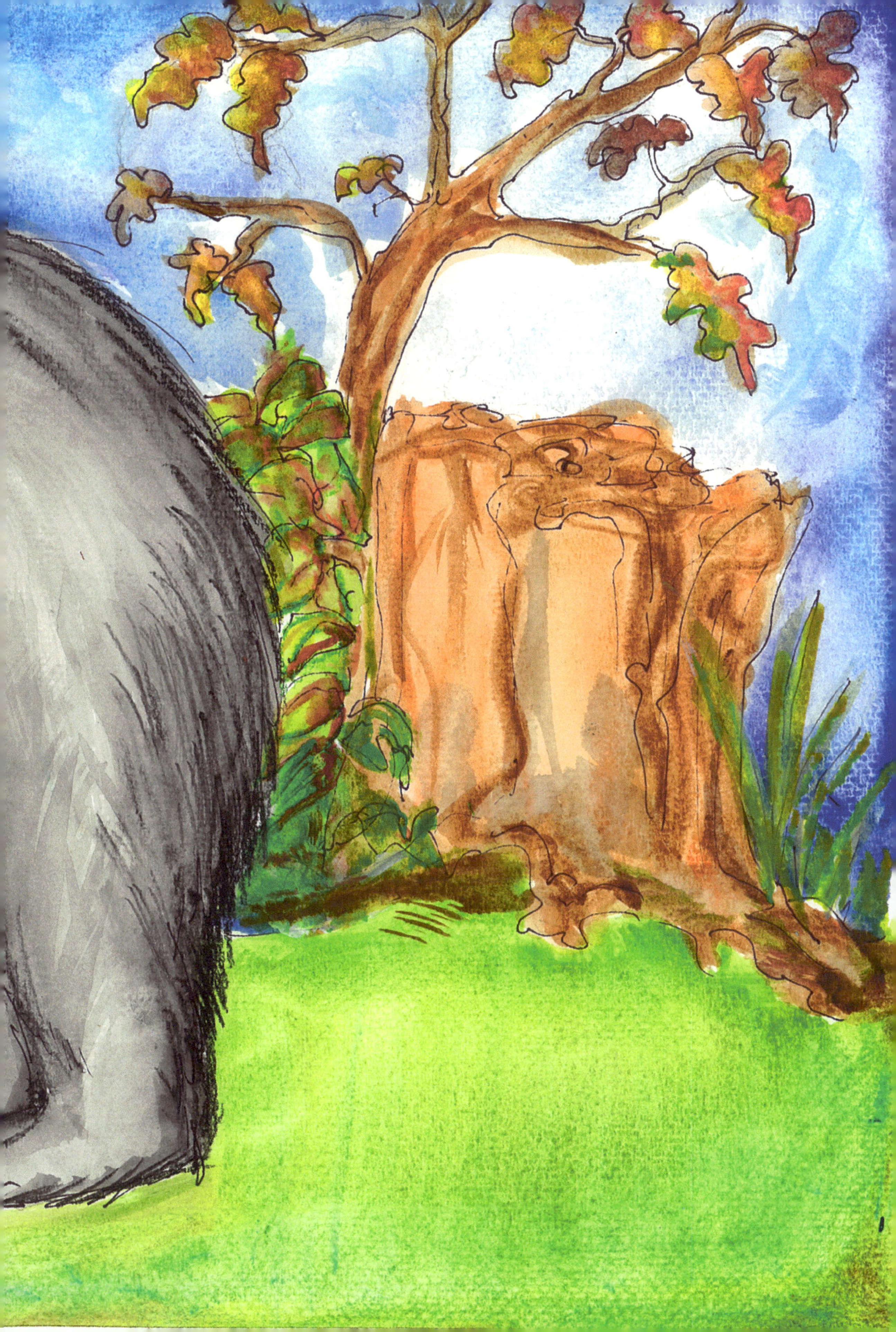

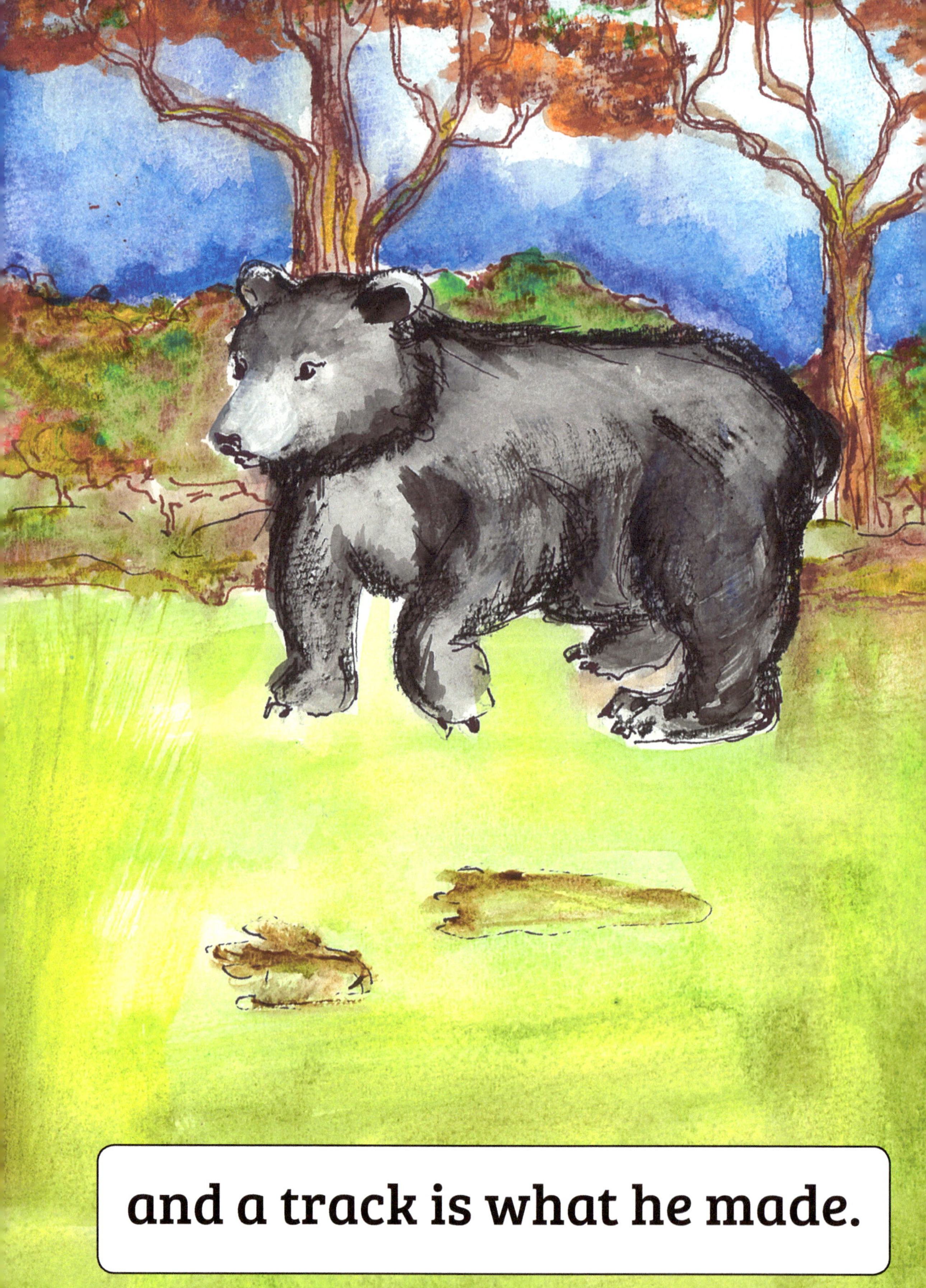

and a track is what he made.

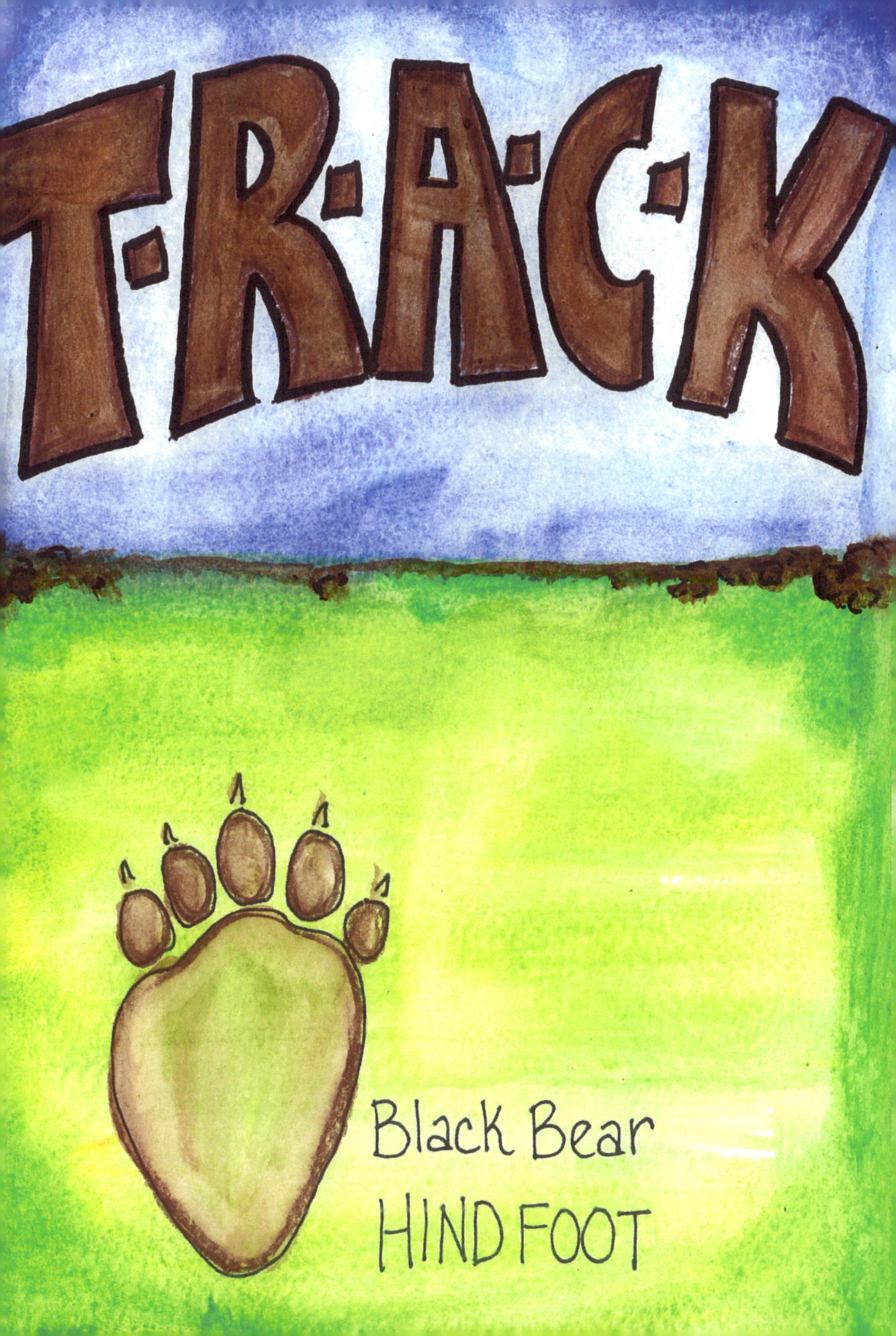

T·R·A·C·K

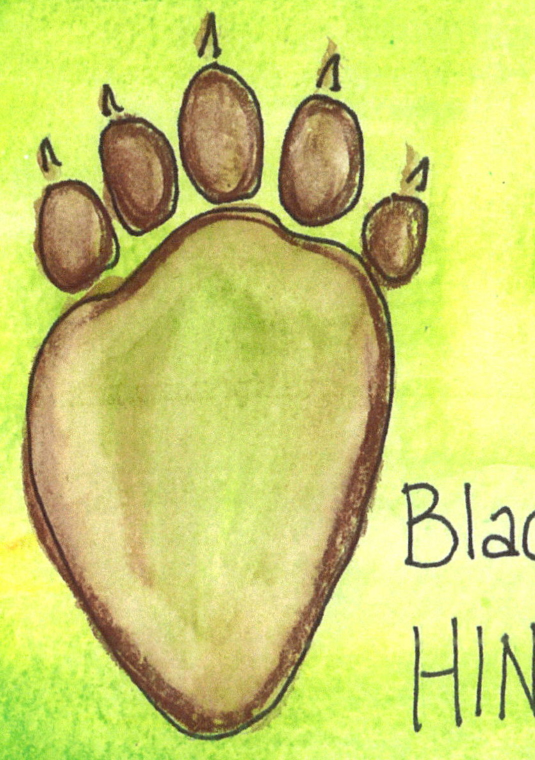

Black Bear
HIND FOOT

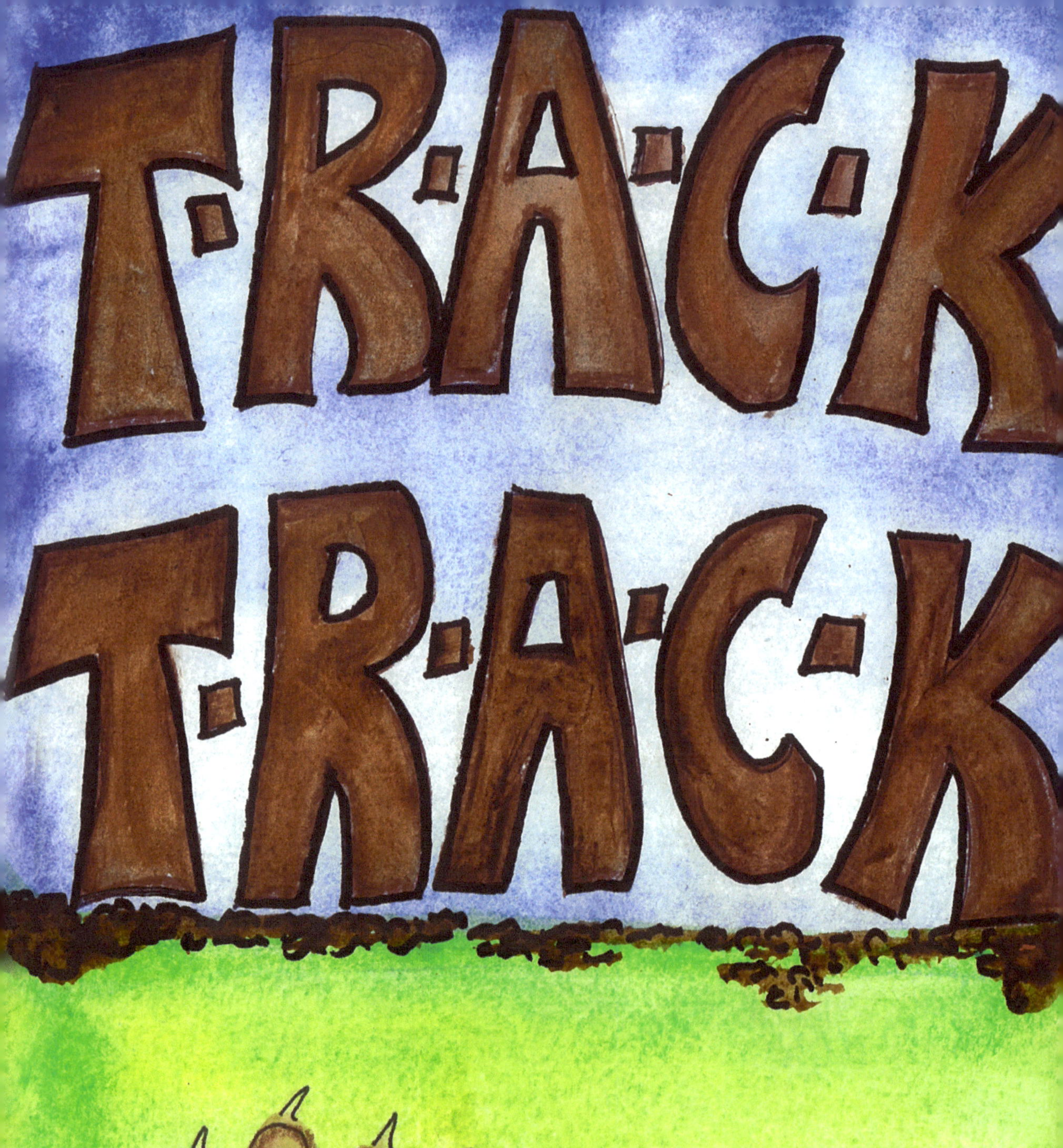

T·R·A·C·K
T·R·A·C·K
Black Bear
FRONT FOOT

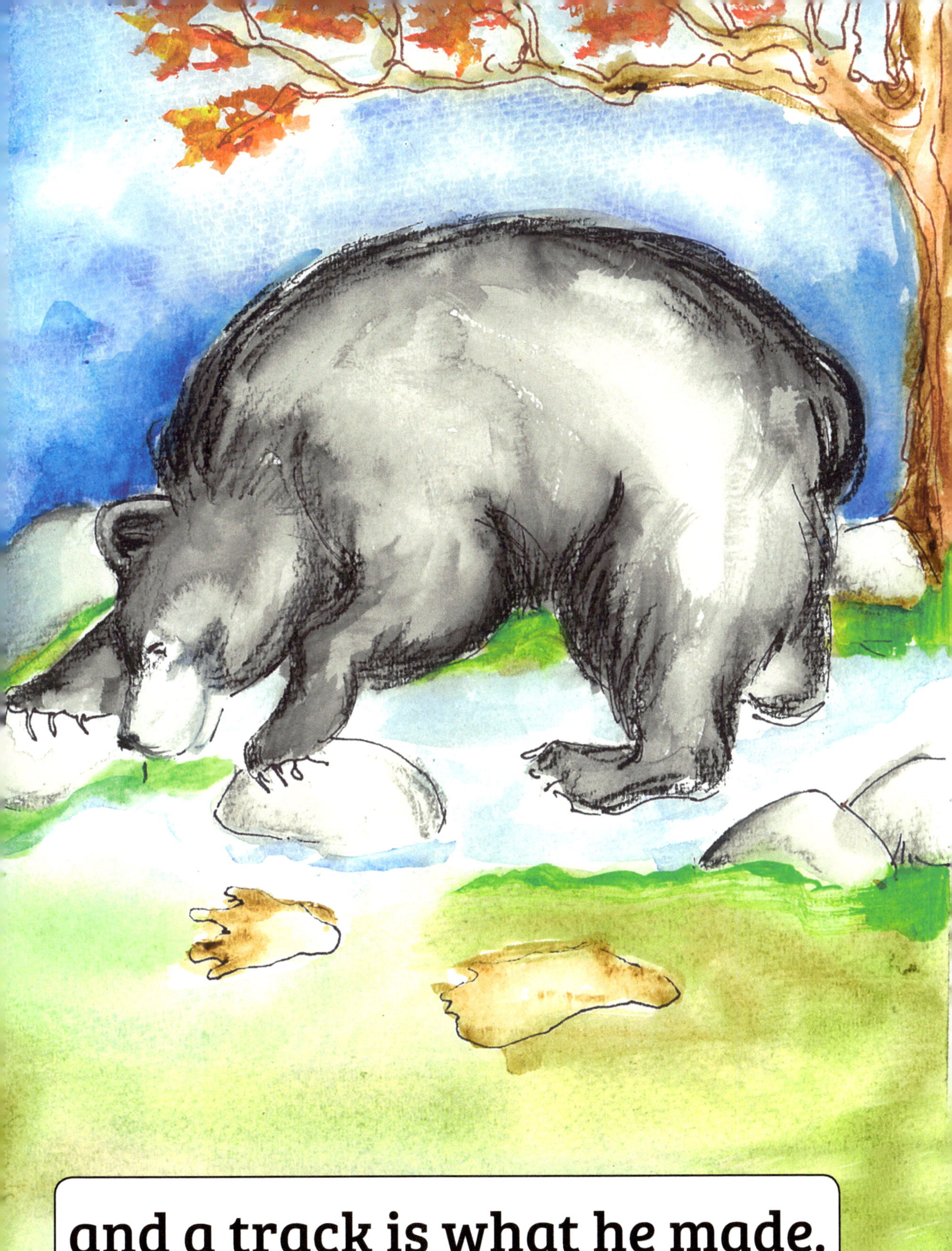

and a track is what he made.

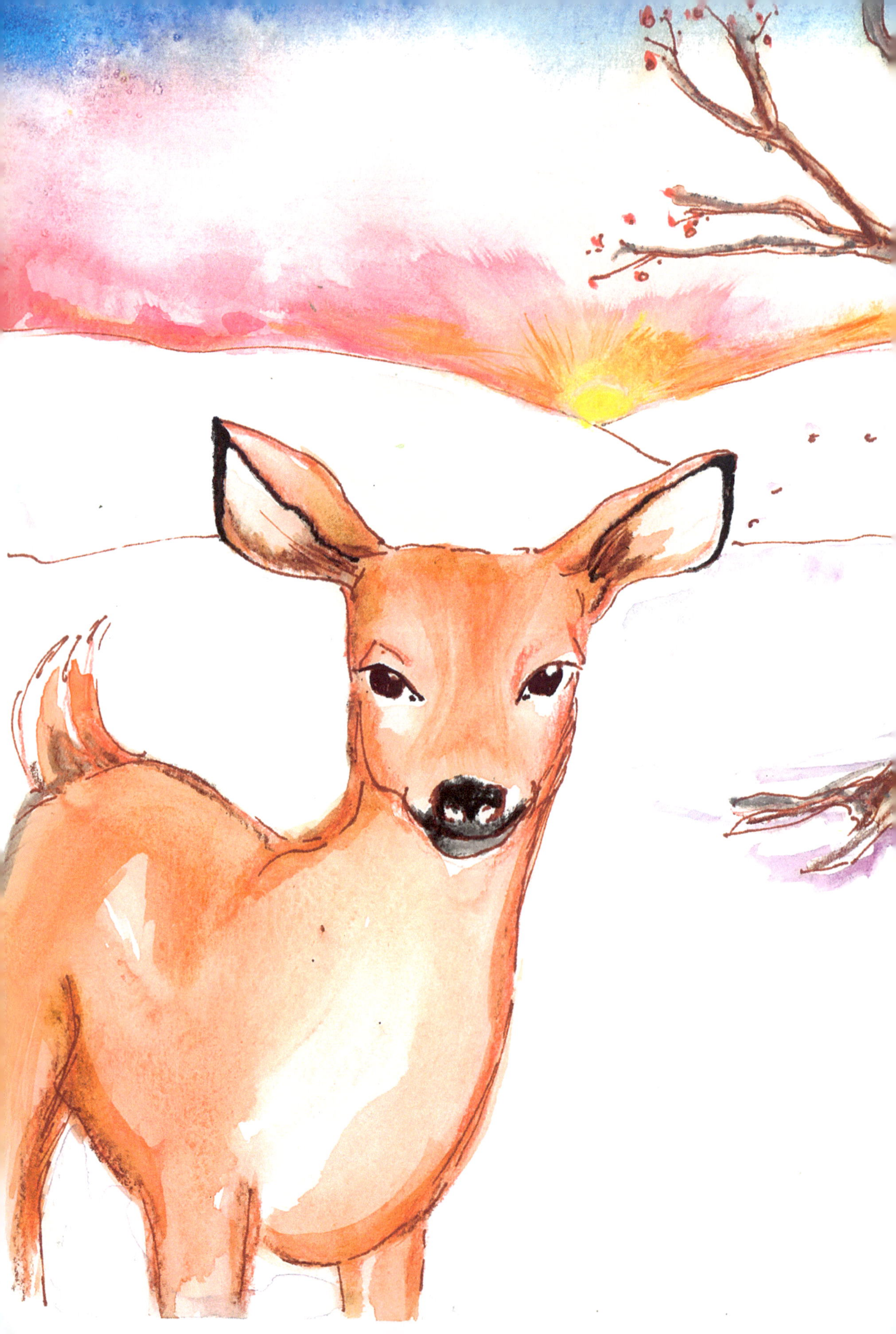

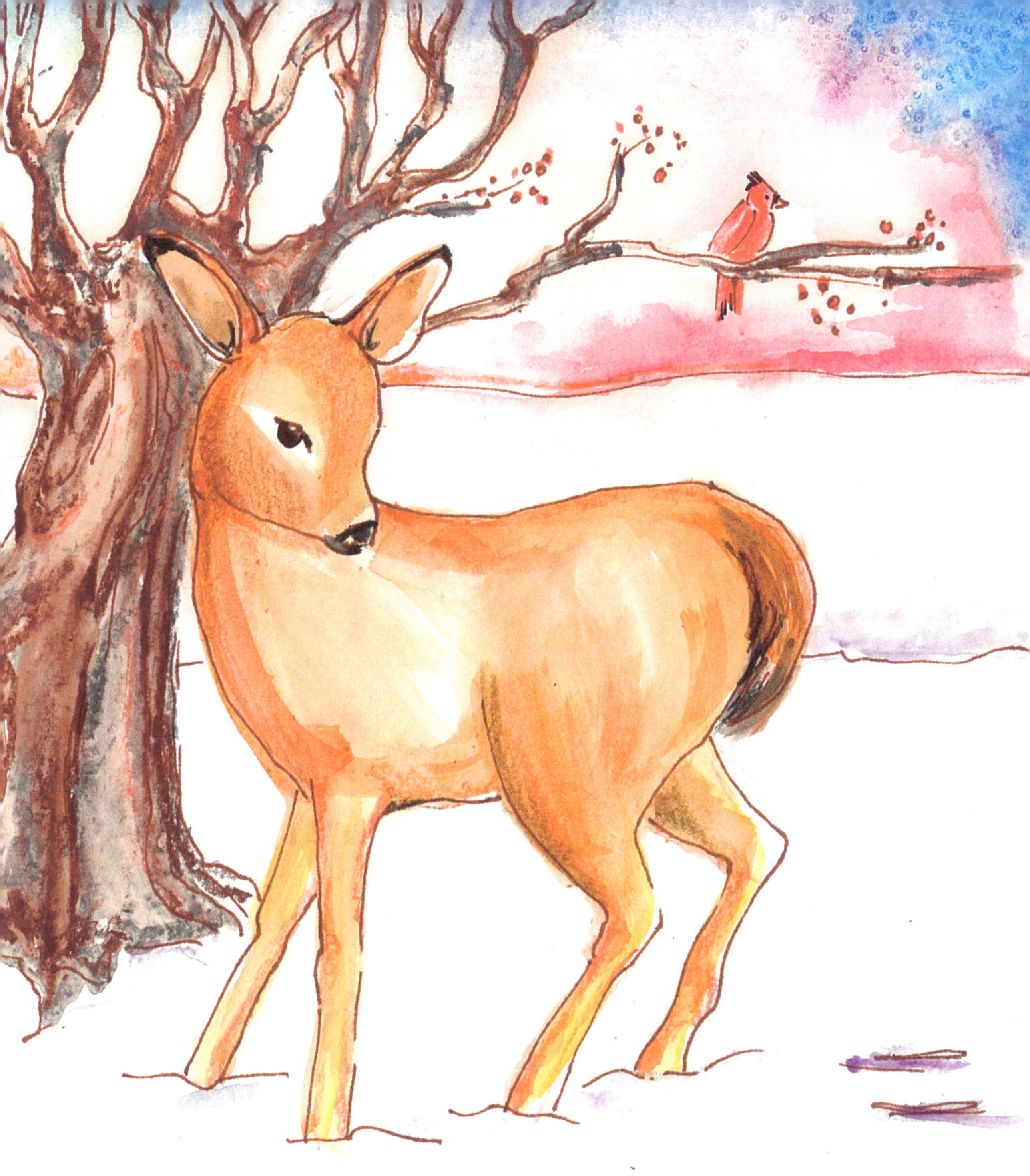

There was a deer that
ran through the snow

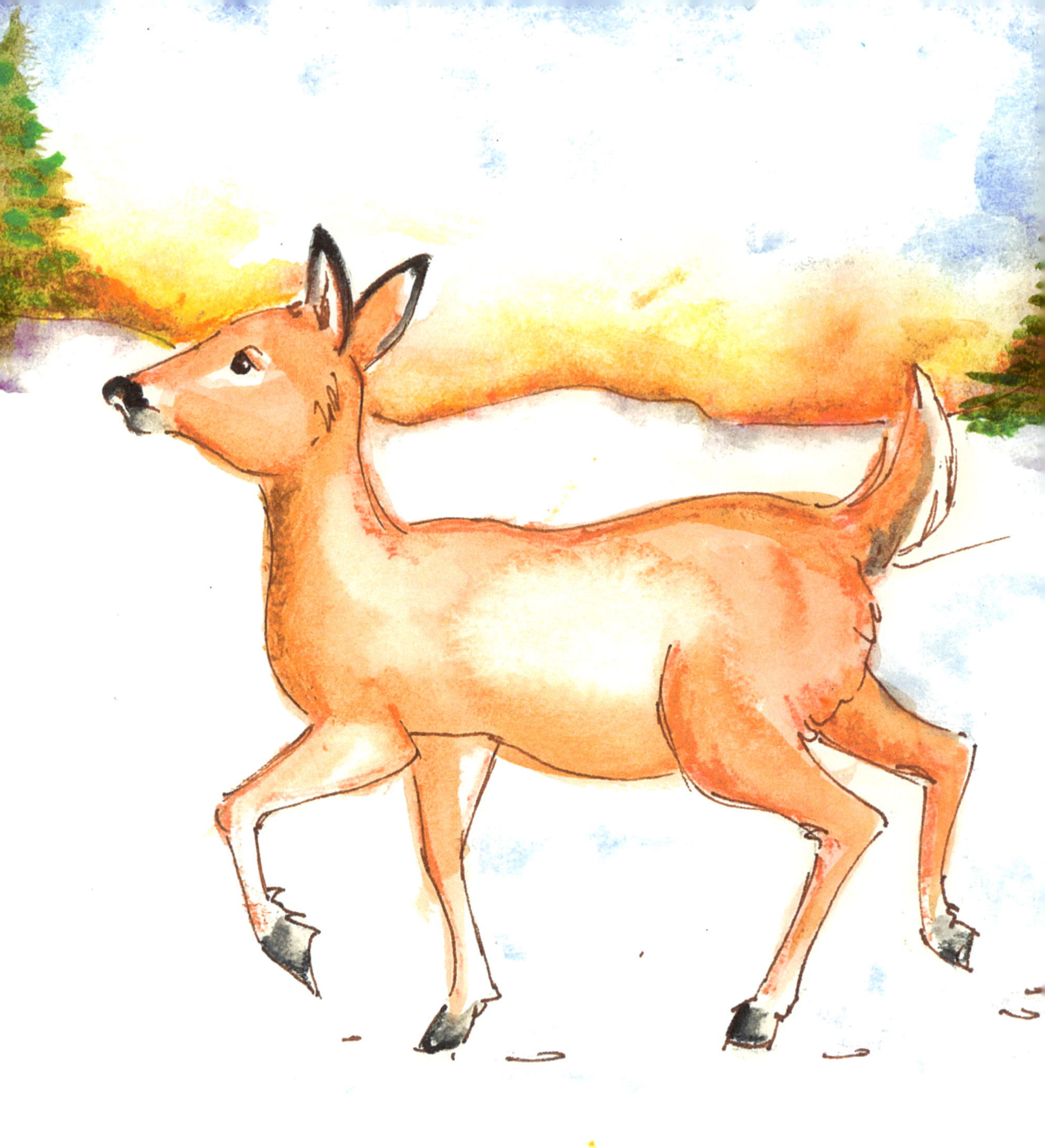

and a track is what she made.

TRACK

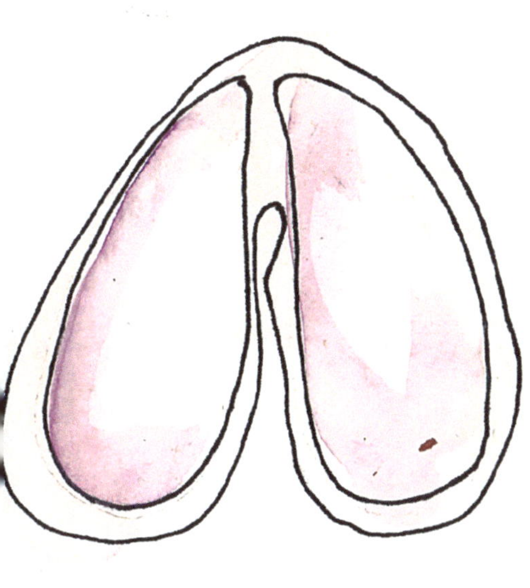

White tailed
Deer
HIND/FOREFOOT

T·R·A·C·K

T·R·A·C·K

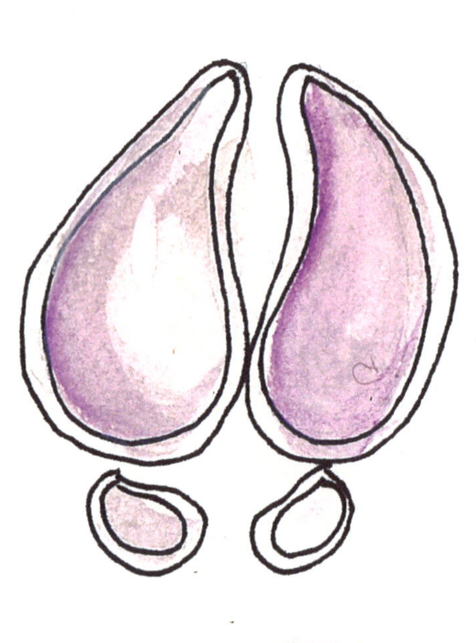

Whitetailed
Deer
RUNNING FEET

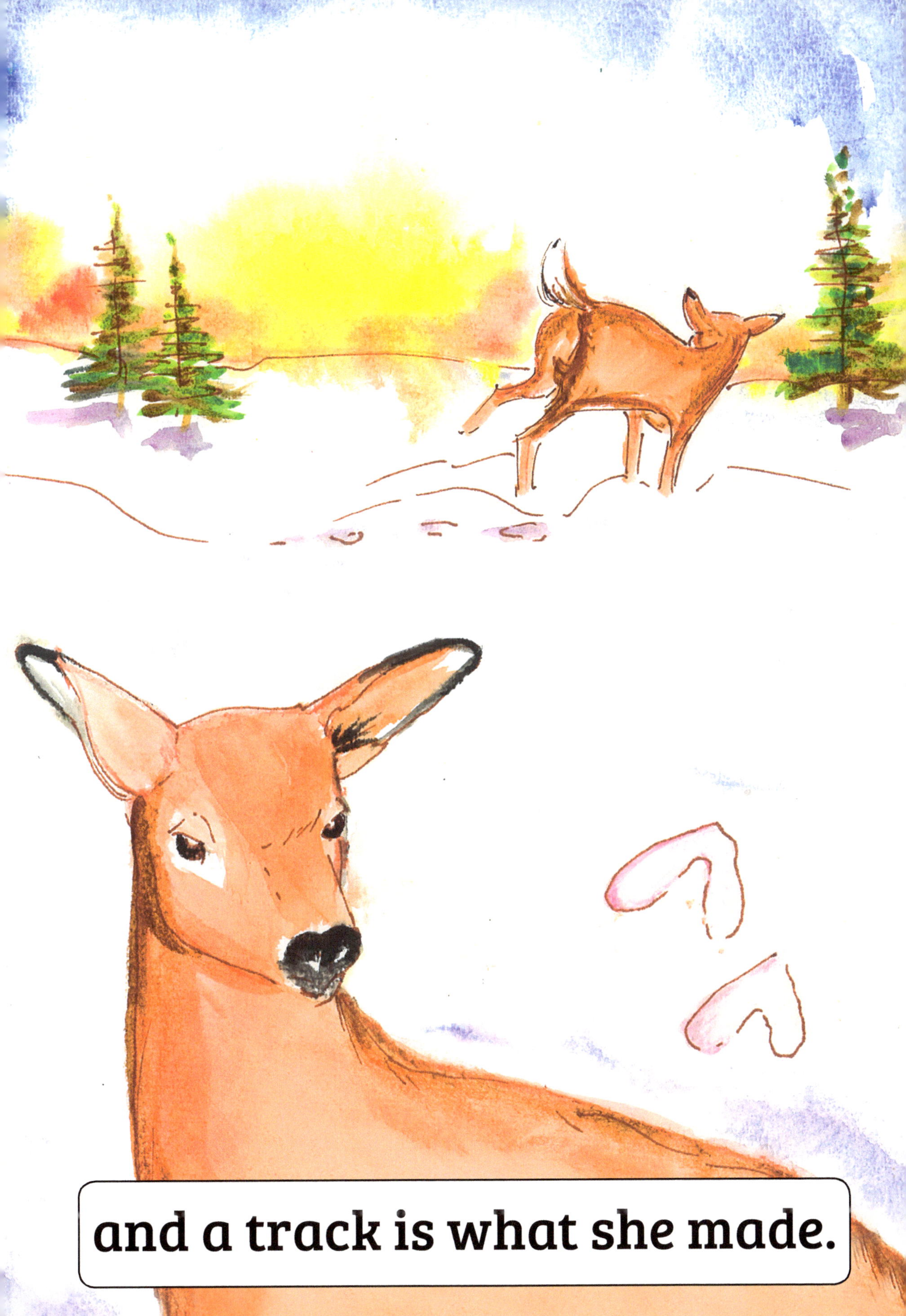

and a track is what she made.

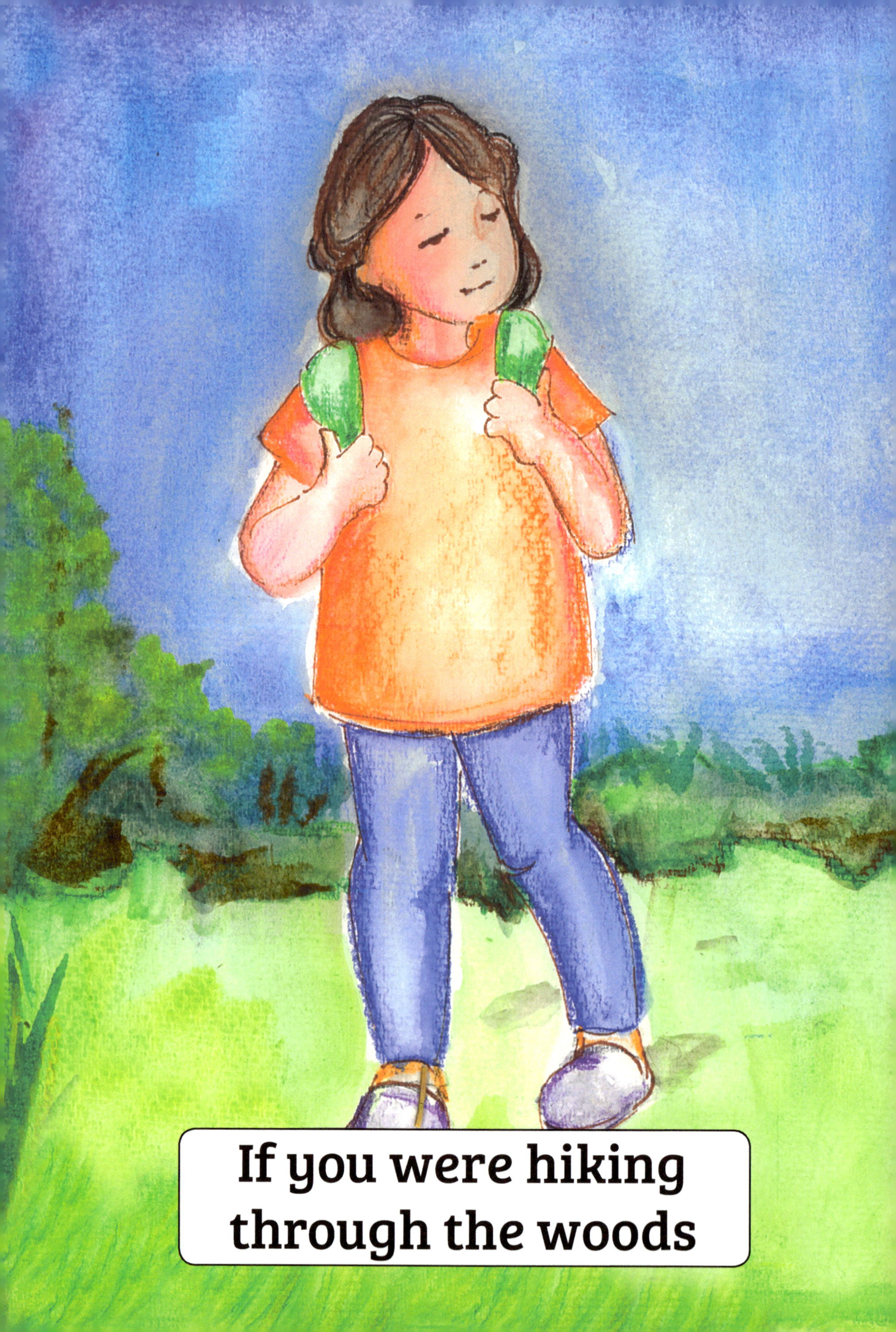
If you were hiking
through the woods

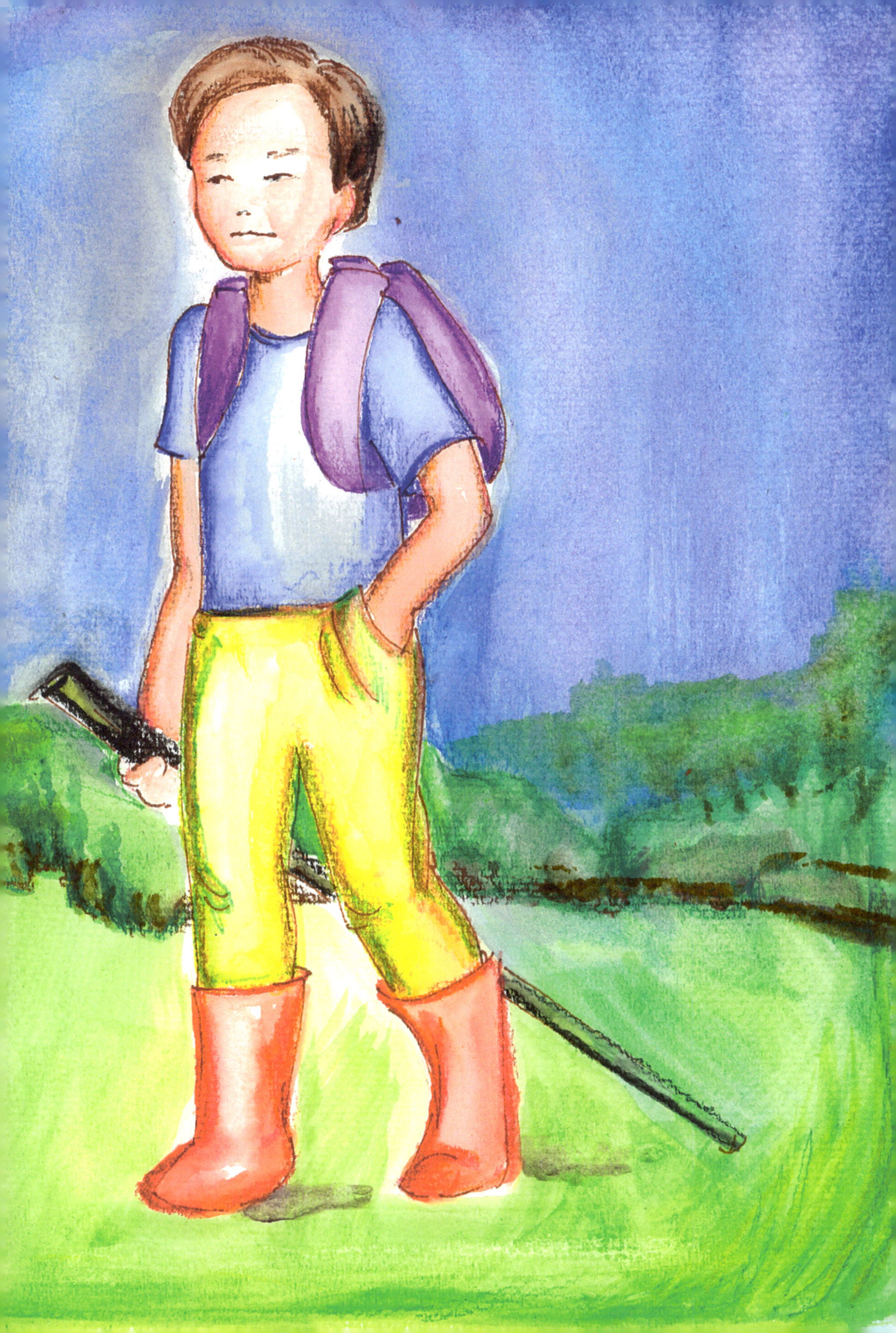

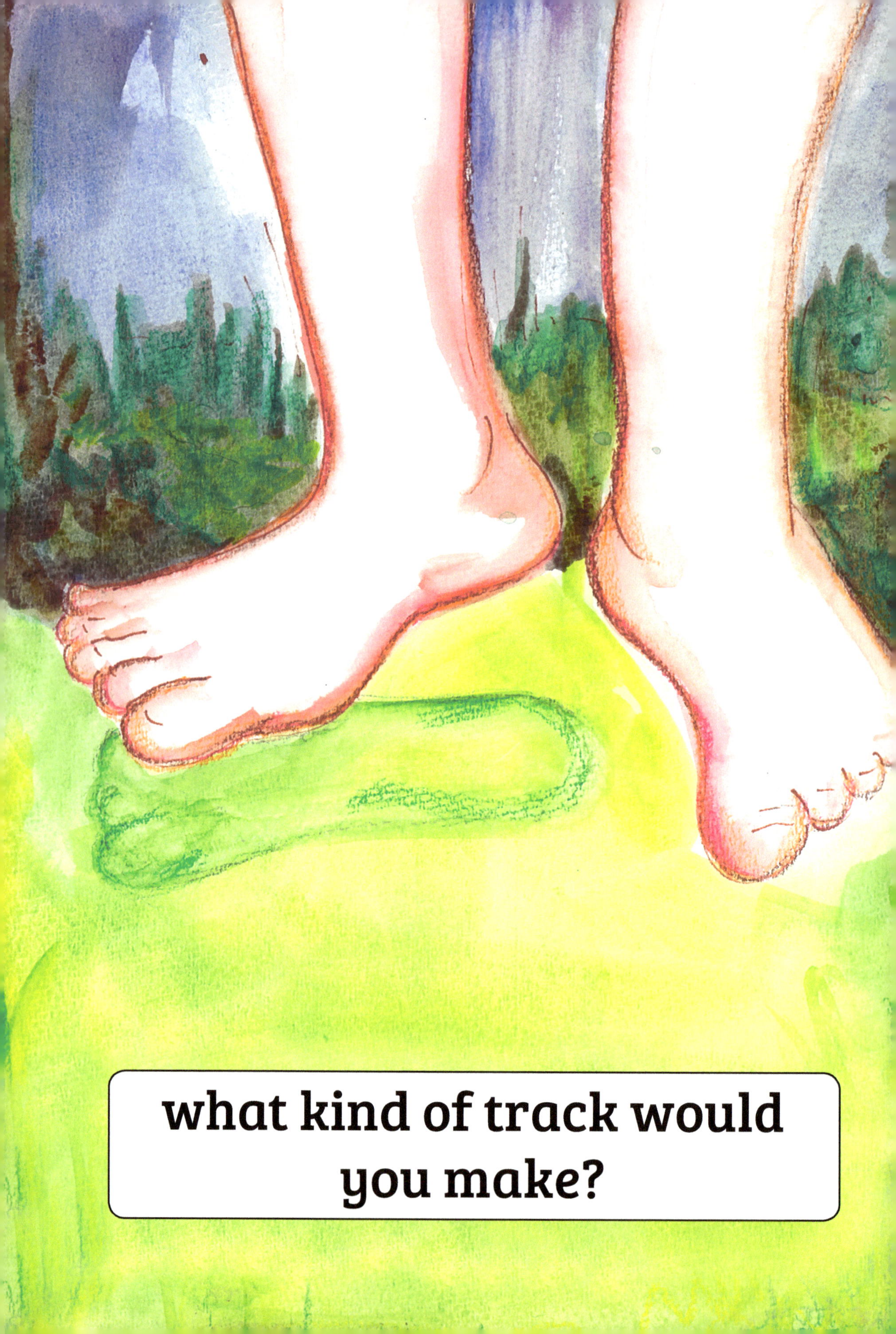

what kind of track would
you make?

T·R·A·C·K

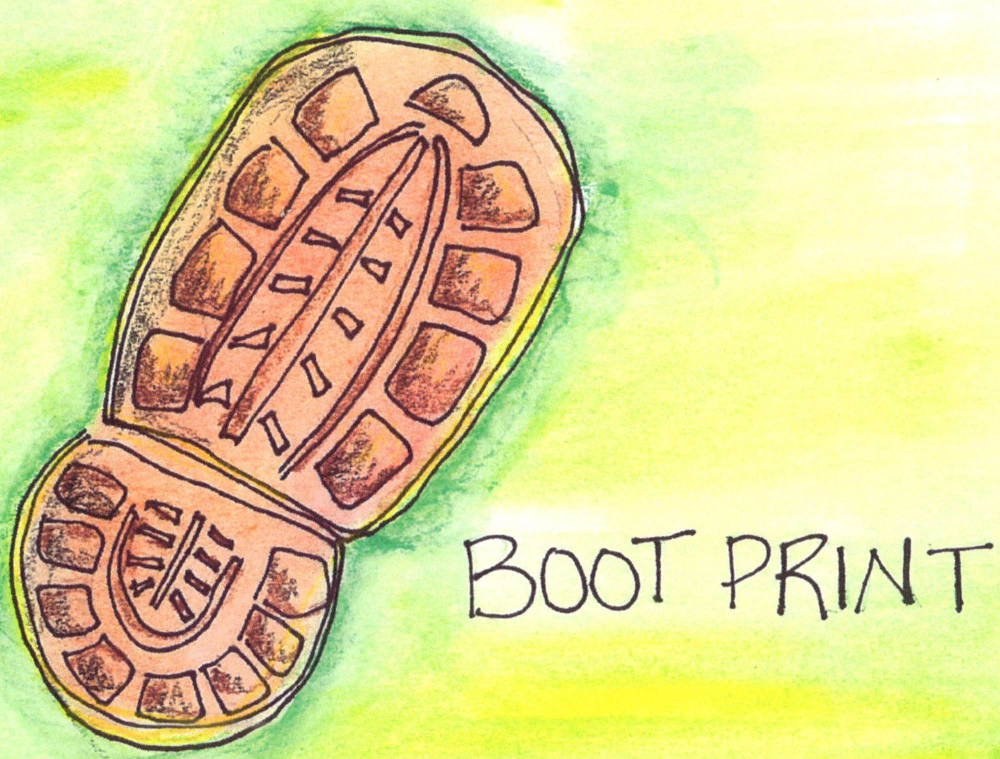

T·R·A·C·K
T·R·A·C·K 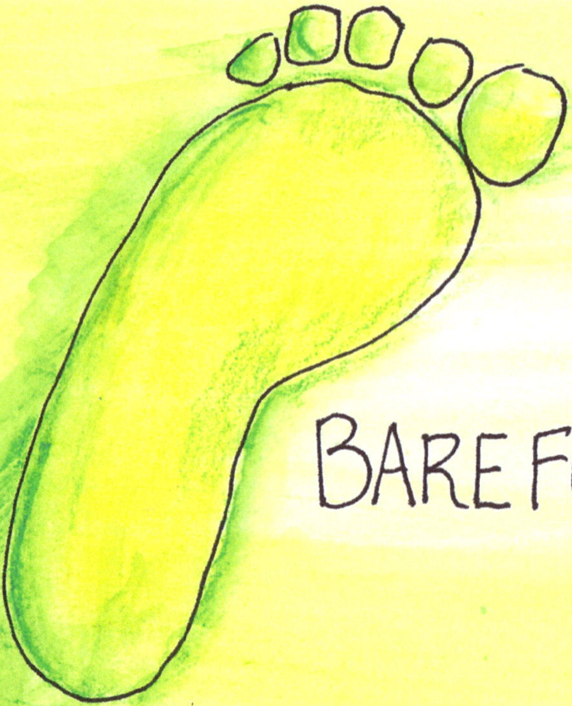
BAREFOOT PRINT

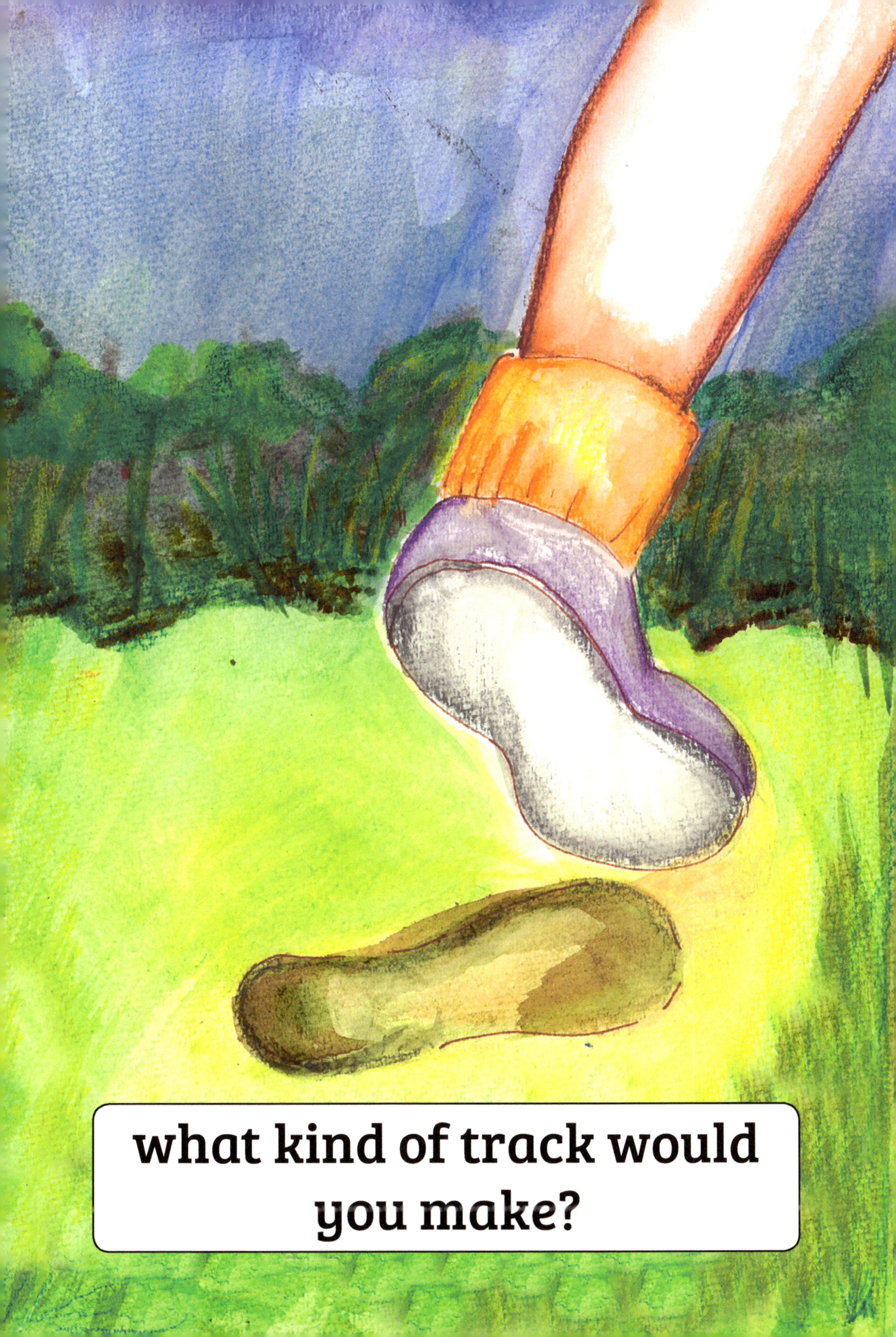

what kind of track would
you make?

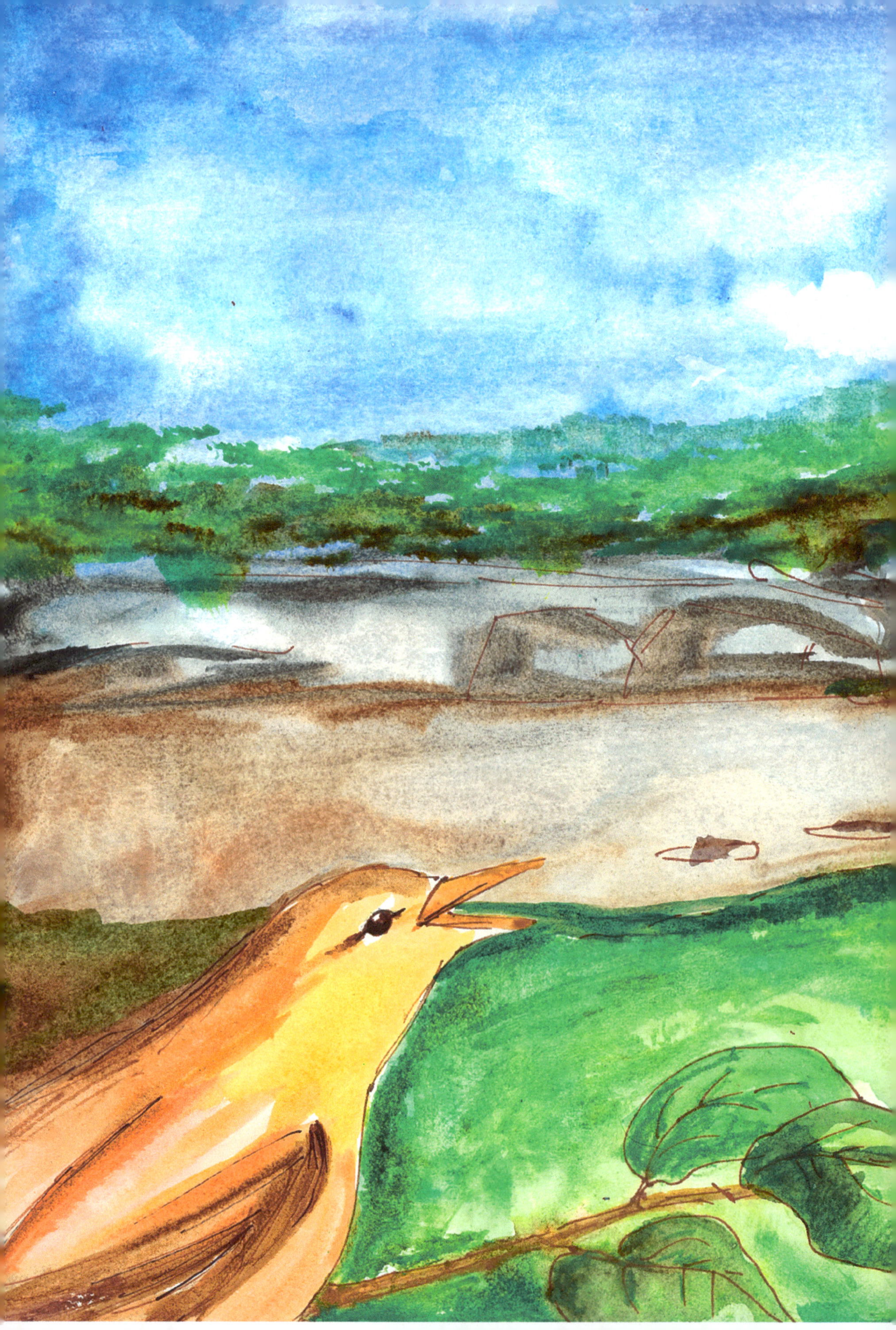

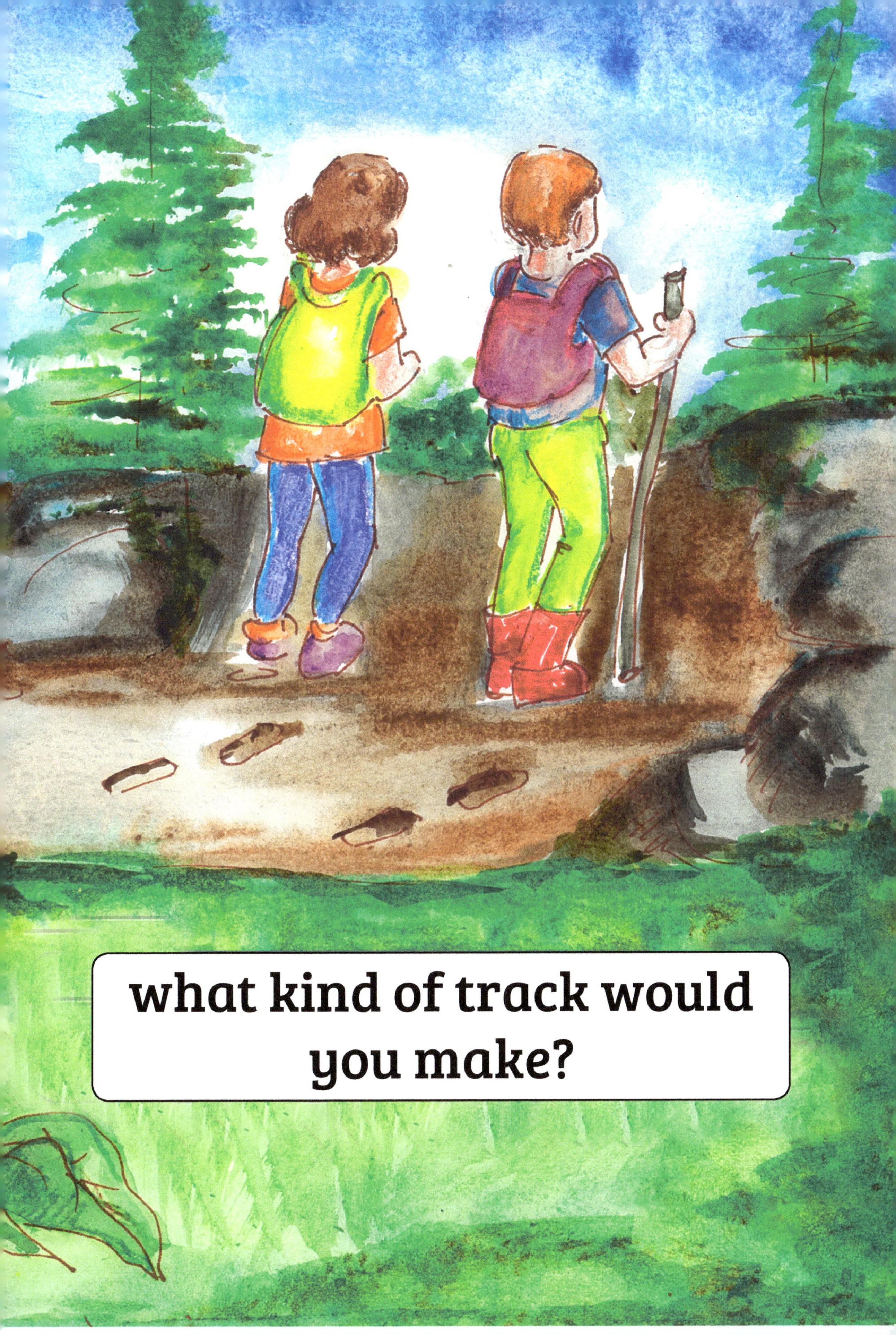

what kind of track would you make?

The End
of the Tracks ...

Re-trace Your Tracks
– A teachers guide to book discussion –

Let's read The Track Song again and see
if you can notice details about:

- Differences in the time of day
- Changes in the seasons
- The types of animals represented
- How and where the tracks are made

Guiding Questions
as you re-trace your tracks:

- Are the tracks different depending on the way the animals move?
- Can you hop, run, shuffle and walk?
- Are the front and back tracks of each animal different or the same?
- Have you ever observed tracks from different animals together? If so, what might this mean?
- Could you tell a story with just tracks? Try it!

What did you like best about
<u>The Track Song?</u>

More Fun With Tracks!

Salt Dough Tracks -

1) Make salt dough recipe.

2) Research animal track images from animal track books or online.

3) Draw or print out the track images. Focus on animals you might find in your local area. Deer, Raccoon, Rabbit, Crow, Squirrel, and even Opossum, might be found in your own backyard.

4) Pat a small lump of salt dough in your hands to fit the size of the animal track. Place the flattened salt dough on a paper plate. Label the plate with the animal name.

5) Using your own fingers, press into the salt dough to mimic the print of the animal track image.

Try using other household items to help you mimic the track from the image into your dough. Example: A Large paperclip might make the mark of a sharp claw in the dough or the foot of a crow. Be Creative.

Once the dough is dry, paint each track with poster paint to make the track impressions more obvious. You may choose to air dry your clay or leave it in your oven on low for about 2 hours.

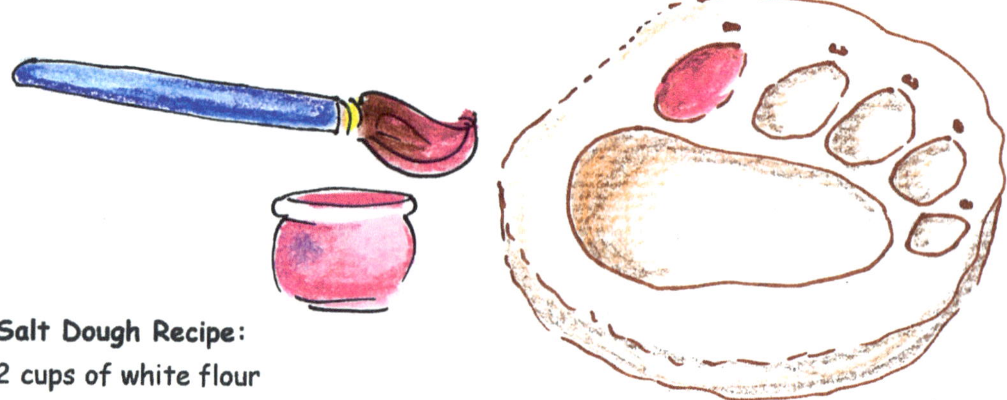

Salt Dough Recipe:

2 cups of white flour

1 cup salt

1 cup water

Mix the dough in a large bowl. It will be sticky. Add a little bit more flour, if needed. It may be used right away or wrapped in foil and stored in your fridge.

Even More Fun With Tracks!

Track Stamping Pads –

Materials:

Construction Paper - Any color
Thick Cardboard (Pizza Round, Shipping Box)
Thin Cardboard (Cereal Box, Gift Box)
Scissors   Glue   Pencil   White Paper - 12X18
Animal Track Books or Printed Animal Tracks copy
Poster Paint and Paintbrush

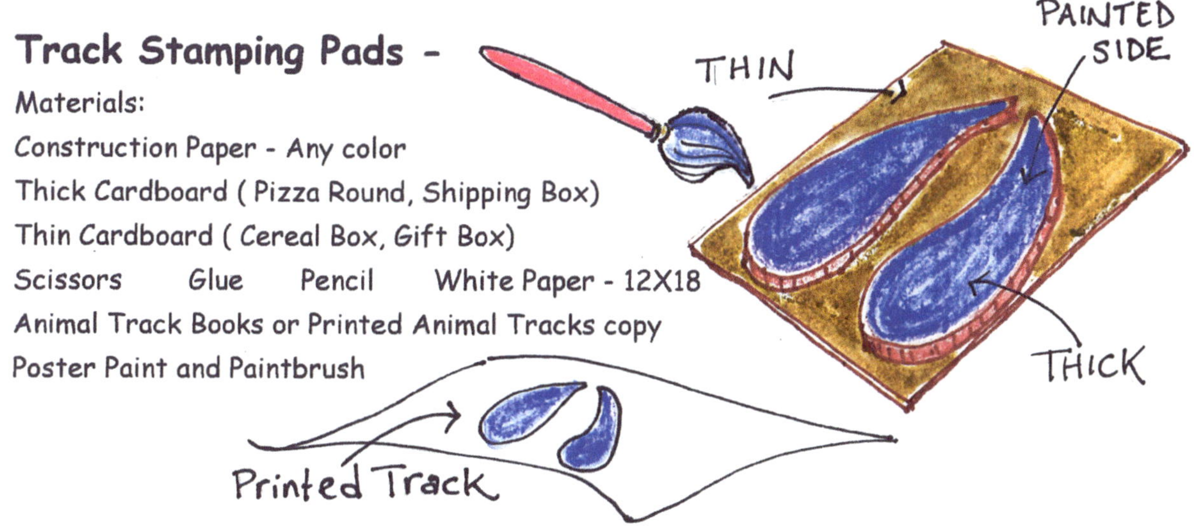

1) Decide which animal tracks you would like to make into a stamp. Choose animals that you might see in your own neighborhood. You might be surprised at which animals decide to roam outside your door! Coyote and Fox will sometimes travel into your own backyard! Once you have decided, draw the animal track on a piece of construction paper. Cut out each of the main parts of the animal track. (Don't worry about including claws, you can paint them on later)

2) Lay the cut out track parts onto the thick cardboard. Again, trace around each part. Next, carefully cut out the thick cardboard track pieces. Arrange them in the correct track pattern onto the thin cardboard. Trace around each of the thick cardboard onto the thin cardboard. Glue each of the thick track parts onto the thin cardboard, carefully matching the outline. Let it dry. (Use this time to begin a second animal track)

3) After the stamp has dried completely, paint the thick cardboard track parts with poster paint. Next, Flip the painted track over and press <u>down</u> the track stamp onto a white piece of paper. Use an even and firm pressure for the best print. Label the track with the animal's name.

You could make your own animal tracks book! Look up facts about each animal. Include some magazine photos of the animal! You will be a Tracking Expert!!

About the Author

Chelsea O'Brien is both the founder and executive director for the non-profit educational farm, The Clarkston Family Farm. Having graduated from WMU's Lee Honor's College with a bachelor's degree in the biological sciences, Chelsea continued her training in health care and also received her environmental educator certification through FSU. Growing up on a large community-based sustainable farm instilled in her a deep love of the natural world and a passion for educating the next generation about the value and joy of growing nutritious food while honoring organic farming practices. Chelsea's passion for experiential learning outdoors drives her to teach and create curriculum and spaces where kids can learn through fun, interactive hands-on experiences in nature.

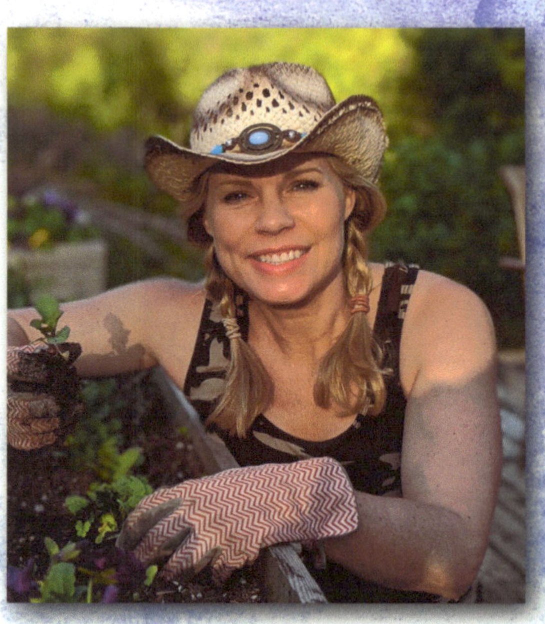

About the Artist

Nancy Berg is a passionate life-long educator who holds both a M.A. Education degree from WMU and an Education Specialist Degree with an Administrator Certification from MSU. Her professional experience includes being a K-12 Art Educator, a Rockford Public Schools elementary teacher and assistant principal for Sparta Middle School. Beyond her 30 years of teaching she has also illustrated a number of children's books and enjoys creating art using a variety of mediums. Illustrations for The Track Song were created using pen, ink and watercolor. Nancy currently serves as curriculum consultant for the Clarkston Family Farm's advisory board.

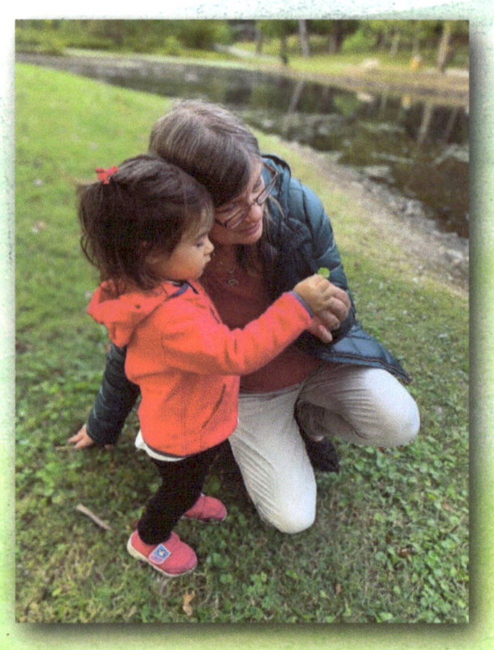

www.ingramcontent.com/pod-product-compliance
Lightning Source LLC
Chambersburg PA
CBHW041134260726
48664CB00026B/667